Editorial

One subscriber, John Looker, enjoyed Colin Bramwell's introductory contribution to *PNR* 283 in Scots. With a parodic Home Counties voice, he said, 'I should be grateful if you would kindly inform Mr Bramwell that I found his essay jolly interesting. Frightfully witty too. I had to read it slowly and, to my shame, rather suspect that my lips were moving but I caught his gist and found myself nodding along.' The linguistic magic worked, it made his lips move to *make* sense. It insisted he turn up the volume of his reading so he could hear what the language was doing, beyond meaning.

Judging from responses to the issue, the challenges it offered will take some time to resolve. *PNR* 284 continues the project – hardly surprising, since much of the content here was commissioned for 283. That issue grew to an impossible extent. Half of 284 is a rich overspill. Another fat issue! – and just when we want to reduce the magazine to a manageable extent for our readers and our finances. The last thing we want to do is raise subscription rates.

PNR 284 is full of revisitings, another term for translation, as well as for the kinds of time travel that memory represents in fragmentary essaylets that can make up a single essay. Sasha Dugdale's 'Benjamin in Moscow' weaves considerations of Meyerhold, Benjamin and of her own experiences of the city over time. 'That was me! I see it now. I stared and stared and could not speak. The future arrived in 1991 and I watched it, but failed to write it. It gradually became the past, and still I failed to write it. And now, by and large, it is barely spoken of, this vital, shame-filled interval between the snarling years.'

Csilla Toldy engages Baudelaire in dialogue: prose or verse? Clearly one, clearly the other. It concludes,

> in turbulent times
> walk on water
> holding hands

Alberto Manguel finds personal histories in libraries, in their content and their intent, in what they reveal about him and about us, then and now. Moments in contemporary history impinge on old or ancient items: police activity in Jerusalem resonates in Bercy, in the National Library of France celebrating its thirtieth anniversary at a time when, once again, books are regarded as provocations. A small, perilous gesture of resistance resonates in an image, translated without loss of meaning across languages and cultures.

And there is Iryna Shuvalova's poem 'written in response to the death, in a Russian air strike, of the Ukrainian writer Victoria Amelina':

> and now only her clothes remain her boots
> the left sole slightly more worn on the inside
> the torn edge of the coat pocket sewn up
> by a hand that
> suddenly no longer knows how to sew
> or write or hold a knife or fork or stroke
> her son's head or click her fingers
> impatiently

Or A.E. Stallings's tight, exemplary quatrains that end,

> Buds are bombs,
> Though when they burst,
> No one is hurt.
> (Or not at first.)

Not at first. Yet a resonance, an effect, begins to build – a potent residue, from the bud as from the bomb. Greg O'Brien and Jenny Bornhold visit Japan and curate an exhibition there which evokes an unfamiliar country and brings its culture into an alien focus. It reveals at least two truths at once, in visual and verbal images.

Whenever I see a new issue *of Modern Poetry in Translation*, a magazine with which *PN Review*'s early years are closely entwined, I think it should be renamed *Modern Poetry Is Translation*. Or has the time come to change the title of this journal, which has always celebrated Babel, to *Poetry Ziggurat Review*? We can dedicate it to Inshushinak, the Bull-God of Susa, among other gods, past and present.

Letter to the Editor

Peter McCarey writes: Given the range of Sergey Zavyalov's poetry it is worth noting that at least one book of his is available in English: *Advent, Leningrad, 1941* (Molecular Press, Geneva, 2017), in a Russian and English parallel text approved by the poet. In spite of the subject matter, its tone is far from the austerity of the classical fragments translated by J. Kates for *PN*. Its distinctive narrative form prompted Robert Crawford's *Curriculum Violette*; it was set to music in a massive oratorio by Sergei Akhunov. There is more on the poet's Wiki page, and more that awaits a talented translator.

News and Notes

The world's oldest literary charity is 235 years old • In 1788 the Revd David Williams set up a fund to 'aid authors in distress', having learned that his friend Floyer Sydenham, an elderly translator of Plato's works, had died penniless in a debtors' prison.

This became the Royal Literary Fund, which has done writers untold good over more than two centuries. Coleridge, Kureishi, John Ash – genre is not an object: quality and need are the criteria. 'Through our hardship grants and education programmes to *WritersMosaic*, our online magazine showcasing UK writers of the global majority, we have supported and worked with thousands of writers over the years.' Edward Kemp, the Fund's chief executive, shares seventy facts about their work, including these ten:

1. At his death in 1956 A.A. Milne left the rights to *Winnie-the-Pooh* to four beneficiaries: his family, Westminster School, the Garrick Club and the Royal Literary Fund.
2. Somerset Maugham, Rupert Brooke, Arthur Ransome and G.K. Chesterton left legacies to the Fund.
3. In 1806, Prince George (later King George IV) was invited to support the Fund and presented it with a house at 36 Gerrard Street, Soho.
4. The RLF digital archive lists every successful and unsuccessful applicant (3662) between July 1790 and November 1939.
5. The tenth applicant was the Chevalier d'Eon, the eighteenth-century soldier, spy and diplomat who 'famously lived openly as a man and then from

1777, presented permanently as a woman. After a falling out with a superior, d'Eon published French diplomatic secrets in *Lettres, memoires et negociations*, one of the most scandalous books of the age'.
6. René de Chateaubriand, exiled in London, was a beneficiary.
7. The first woman to benefit (several times) from grants was Charlotte Lennox, Scottish author of *The Female Quixote* (1752).
8. The RLF's Bridge programme of workshops was devised by novelist and memoirist Katie Grant to bridge the learning gap between school and university. Today, the Bridge team consists of sixty-four writers working in secondary schools, sixth-forms and further-education colleges across the UK. RLF Bridge Fellows have worked in some 800 schools and colleges, reaching over 30,000 students.
9. The longest-serving RLF Secretary was Octavian Blewitt, who joined the Fund in 1839, the year Charles Dickens became part of the committee: they did not always see eye-to-eye: Dickens called Blewitt 'the Pious Octavian' and 'the Blessed Blewitt'.
10. Dickens had a tumultuous relationship with the RLF. He became Steward of the annual dinner in May 1837, was elected to the Committee in 1839, then barred from re-election for non-attendance.

A chill wind for global literature • *The editors of the American magazine* Agni *wrote on 8 May:* 'It's the common refrain right now, unfortunately: We've lost our Federal support. It's true of so many who were working toward a stable new life in this country; it's true of many who were fighting disease and food insecurity both here and abroad; it's true of nearly everyone who proved the value of their work in civil rights or climate change to government agencies that once proudly supported them. It's true of *Agni* now as well. It happened in the way we've come to expect this year: on a Friday night, after the week's news cycle went quiet.'

The editors declared their intention to continue – a possibility which the demands on private charity may make impossible: 'despite these challenges, we stand firm in our mission to amplify global literary voices and invite readers to explore a wider world through literature. This setback only strengthens our belief in the power of international literature, and our dedication to the community of readers, writers, and translators we serve.' *Agni* was founded in 1972 and is more or less coeval with *PNR*.

Hollowed-out leadership • Andy Croft, poet and editor-publisher of the late lamented Smokestack Books, has published an anthology entitled *Sausages! A new anthology of poems in celebration of Sir Keir Starmer KC*. This is much more distinctive than the e-book *Poems for Corbyn* of 2015. That anthology included commissioned poems. By contrast, this collection 'brings together 50 poets to mark the absence and emptiness of the current Labour leadership. The result is a kind of hollowed-out cultural artefact – fitting, we thought – that uses the form of an anthology to explore the space where vision, hope, commitment and meaning used to be.' The poem is free from the Culture Matters website.

The Poetry Business at forty: Ann and Peter Sansom celebrate a milestone year • The Sheffield-based publisher The Poetry Business has reached the age of forty and deserves a loud bravo. Its journal *The North*, its books and pamphlets, its writer development work, its resilience when faced with crises of various kinds, make it a unique presence. It insists on its Yorkshireness. It thrives in Sheffield because of that city's 'strong sense of community': poets attend each others' readings, share information and advice, celebrate peers' successes, everyone is supportive. 'That's a very Sheffield trait', said Peter Sansom. 'We let people into traffic here, rather than pushing our own way in! Poets are very proud of this collaborative and collegiate approach. It often exists in places where there have been hard times – it's an ethical attitude hardwired into people. Maybe that's why Sheffield is a city of sanctuary.'

The publisher – with its Smith|Doorstop imprint – dates from Peter's days as research assistant at Huddersfield Polytechnic. 'The Enterprise Allowance was offering £40 per week to get small businesses off the ground, so a lot of arts operations took advantage of that. I started in a Victorian arcade in the centre of Huddersfield, where there was a lovely attic office at a peppercorn rent. I'm not sure I really had any plans, my own first book had just been accepted, and I knew I loved poems and working with poets.' That love has continued unabated. The imprint is responsible for more than a thousand titles. Its annual International Book and Pamphlet Competition is popular and it runs a hundred workshops a year. A recent project was *The Coal Anthology*, marking the fortieth anniversary of the miners' strike. Ann Samson said, 'Peter and I are both from mining families, so that project meant a huge amount to us. We feel strongly about being able [...] to run events in libraries and other venues in places such as Selby, Barnsley or Rotherham where there might not always be much access to poetry. Five years ago, class was barely mentioned in publishing circles, so it's good that it's getting talked about more.' Poetry is not a rewarding business for most. 'Occasionally it crosses our minds what it would be like to have a "proper" job or a pension, but it's usually only a fleeting thought. What we do is exciting and we get to work with interesting people and feel like we're doing something meaningful. It's really important to believe the work you do makes a difference.'

Faultlines of modernity • *John McAuliffe writes:* The Irish poet Paul Durcan has died, aged eighty. Durcan's poems knew intimately the Irish hierarchies they mercilessly surfaced and sent up for five decades: he grew up in Ranelagh in Dublin, and had a difficult relationship with his father, a Circuit Court judge and the subject of coruscating poems. Durcan had been committed to a mental institution as a young man and did not complete his undergraduate studies at University College Dublin, but was part of a group of young poets, including Eiléan Ní Chuilleanáin and Michael Hartnett, who gathered around

Patrick Kavanagh in his final years. While publishing his first books, he was a mature student, having returned to University College Cork to study Archaeology.

Those books, *O Westport in the Light of Asia Minor* (1975), *Teresa's Bar* (1976) and *Sam's Cross* (1978), establish an everyday surrealism in their angular descriptions, offering alternative news headlines about contemporary Irish life and including entirely characteristic, now-famous anthology pieces, 'Making Love Outside Áras an Uachtaráin', 'The Death by Heroin of Sid Vicious' and 'Tullynoe: Tête-à-Tête in the Parish Priest's Parlour'. Subsequent books would include *Jumping the Train Tracks with Angela* (co-published by Raven Arts Press and Carcanet in 1983), *Daddy, Daddy* (1986) for which he won the Whitbread Prize, and a pair of ekphrastic books, *Crazy about Women* (1991) and *Give Me Your Hand* (1994), which invented monologues for the figures he found in both the London and Dublin National Galleries. Later books included the long poem *Christmas Day* (1997), *Greetings to Our Friends in Brazil* (1999) and a serviceably extensive selected poems, *Life is a Dream* (2009).

Durcan's work was attentive to the faultlines which modernity and prosperity exposed in Ireland. The poems both lovingly enumerate and relish mocking the hypocrisies he saw everywhere around him, and the work was at the heart of debates about revisionist history and Ireland's modernization, with Edna Longley, Colm Tóibín and Niall McMonagle either editing selections or writing about his work and its impact. An astonishing performer of his own work, he held audiences spellbound wherever he read. He was, alongside Brendan Kennelly and Rita Ann Higgins, one of a group of poets who were popular media figures. *Paul Durcan's Diary* (2003) collects his weekly radio broadcasts on Ireland's main current affairs programme.

Durcan was a founding member of Aosdána and was Ireland Chair of Poetry (2004–07). His inimitable voice can be heard to great effect in 'In the Days Before Rock'n'roll', a duet with Van Morrison on the 1990 album, *Enlightenment*.

Nothing but a poet • In May the American poet Alice Notley died at the age of eighty. She was one of the second-generation New York poets, an identification she resisted along with other labels, though she was undeniably the widow and literary executor of Ted Berrigan. Her own experimentation was different in kind from his, moving towards reinvention of conventional forms (metre, for example), but transformed. She developed the conversation form with other, earlier individuals and practitioners, including her late husband. In some ways she resembles Bernadette Mayer, though it is hard to imagine confusing their work. She prospered from collaboration, creative and editorial. The author of more than forty books, chapbooks and pamphlets, she said of herself, in the third person, 'She has never tried to be anything other than a poet'.

Semantic frugality • On 8 July the American poet, novelist and essayist Fanny Howe died. Howe has been a presence in the margins of *PN* Review, having contributed one poem – in 2004 – 'House without Pity', in her pared down lines characteristic of that period. She has appeared in essays by Marjorie Perloff and others, with an essay-length appraisal by Donald Kane (also in 2004) which concludes, 'In many ways Howe stands alone as an American poet in her commitment to dealing with the "old-fashioned", if by old-fashioned we are referring to a poet's self-conscious exploration and evocation of a peculiarly religious vision. Howe's link to American nineteenth-century transcendentalism; her alignment to a Western religious tradition that we can trace back to the work of Renaissance poets as well as to later writers including Gerard Manley Hopkins and perhaps even Eliot; and her displays of innovative poetic form add up to make Fanny Howe a necessary and original figure in contemporary American poetry.' In 2022 Ian Pople dwelt in a *PNR* essay on her conversion to Roman Catholicism (her sister Susan went in the other direction, towards Protestantism) and its thematic and poetic consequences, insisting on her importance. A correspondent in 2014 described her as having 'alarming affinities' with the school of E.J. Thribb – due apparently to her short lines, semantic frugality and unironic manner. Her life, like her writing, risked challenging norms and her work was described as 'a continual transition' in formal and thematic terms.

Beyond commonplace values • The translator Angela Livingstone has died at the age of ninety. Masha Karp wrote on her life and work in the *Guardian* (22 June). Livingstone, as teacher and translator, was 'known for playing a key role in making the most innovative works of twentieth-century Russian literature accessible to the English-speaking world. Her publications include edited selections of writings by Boris Pasternak and Marina Tsvetaeva and masterful translations of their prose and poetry, among them Tsvetaeva's "lyrical satire" *The Ratcatcher* and verse-drama *Phaedra*. [...] She also published *Pasternak: Modern Judgements* (1969), a groundbreaking book of critical essays (in collaboration with the poet and critic Donald Davie), a monograph on Pasternak's *Doctor Zhivago* (1989) and, late in her life, a collection of her own poems, *Certain Roses* (2017).' Elaine Feinstein, Tsvetaeva's best-loved English translator, reviewed *Phaedra*: her version 'not only extends our understanding of a great Russian poet, but also illuminates the spirit of her translator, who is as little interested in the commonplace values of the everyday world as the poet she translates'.

Reports

Listening to Billie Holiday in the Poustinia

ANTHONY VAHNI CAPILDEO

The marguerites open their eyes wide and sway at the side of the path. The scent of grass, sharp and sappy, wanders into the air with the confidence that neither rain nor sun will exert fury on plant life during the growing season. I am in the poustinia, which at its origins means 'desert' in Russian, but in the Eastern Orthodox tradition and beyond has grown to refer to a simple dwelling where the poustinik stays alone in the presence of God. This poustinia, a converted garden shed in the grounds of a community in the Fenlands, has become my favourite place to write, think and sleep.

This morning, we celebrated the feast of St Boniface. Children are great false etymologists; the name 'Boniface' sounded like 'bony face', and I used to attach the same giggling awe to this eighth-century martyr as I did to Great Danes and other gaunt and severe creatures, even though the French and Spanish and Latin of the household made it impossible to ignore that 'Boniface' is a name of doing – face, faire, hacer, facere – not a name of becoming bones, but of doing good. Not to say that our bones do not do; walking along the road, an older Sister encouraged me to forge ahead, because she could go only as fast as her bones would carry her. Not for her Gerard Manley Hopkins's lamentation that 'Man's mounting spirit in his bone-house, mean house dwells' – not unless we take 'mean' as measure and as means. The Spirit's blade hovers with changeless alacrity to cut the cloth, while the metres of the fabric of our journey take their measure from the capacity in our bones. The homilist told us about St Boniface, and how he cut down the mighty thunder oak worshipped by pagans. This baffles me. Is it ever good to cut down trees? What if humans were feeding blood to their roots?

Returned to the poustinia, from my desk I can look into the green-gold and wine-purple leaves of nearby shrubs, and the blue-green of a cypress. To my left, there are a few cherry-pink carnations in a vase in front of an unpainted statue of the Virgin and child. I remember that the child she is holding so calmly while he looks up and pulls hard but lovingly at her hair is the same child she would walk with to his execution; if I turned around, there is an unpainted crucifix in dark wood at my back. Christ was taken down from that tree. A wordless movement, between hurt and thought, spirals in my heart. I need to listen to Billie Holiday, singing 'Strange Fruit'.

1939, a date famous for other reasons, was the year Billie Holiday first recorded a version of 'Strange Fruit', the anti-lynching song primarily written by Abel Meeropol (1903–86), the American son of Ukrainian-Jewish immigrants.

'Listening to Billie Holiday in the poustinia' could be the title for an unwritable memoir.

Billie Holiday sings with terrible calm and beauty. She delivers the lines about the pastoral and gallant south with a face that has life skills. It could pull itself into a graceful, marketable tribute act to this gone-with-the-wind, essence-of-magnolia myth. If the singer wanted to succeed unproblematically. If she needed to 'pass' in polite society. If, like for her ancestors, survival depended on it. A whole other meaning for 'courtesy performance'. The mask stretches but will not break, as the song widens into lamentation. How do we contemplate the 'bulging eyes' and 'twisted mouth' of the Black people 'hanging from the poplar trees'? This is not the poetry of modernism, where shell shock and brain fever sift into broken images. It is not the mid-century sense of the absurd or grotesque in the failure of the human soft machine. For all its vividness, in Billie Holiday's rendition this is an understated song. What statement is not understatement, in the face of such excessive violation? The listener cannot switch off by settling into a groove of vicarious sharing in accusation, or description. For the singer stands in solidarity with the people reduced to a 'crop' of bodies. She carries them. They carry her. They are tender and appalling family.

I am listening to Billie Holiday in the poustinia because I have been reading James H. Cone, *The Cross and the Lynching Tree* (2011). His book makes me feel sane. He writes the things that I thought had to remain unspoken. Growing up in Trinidad and in my family, I had benefitted from a good education in high culture. This meant that almost everything I read or that I was taught, I heard antiphonally, or like a call and response, or as if it featured speech bubbles, marginalia, or subtitles. Everything had extras unintended by the authors – no narrative was so masterful, no information so mainstream, as to arrive in my mind without the withheld (not untold) story, the oral history, the ancestral tradition, the outright contradiction, the knowledge of other knowledge. Sometimes a facial expression, sometimes a tone of voice, sometimes an open comment from an adult – not always a 'teacher', not always 'educated' or 'in charge' – opened the way. Sometimes you had to be told at length. These things, you knew, were not to be written in exams. Not if you wanted to pass.

James H. Cone writes aloud all this commentary into his academic prose. How and why did white preachers, academics, and so many others not make the connection between the cross and the lynching tree? How, with the prophetic witness of Harlem Renaissance poets and musicians? It feels like stepping out of a dangerously out of control vehicle and sitting on a bench, recovering orientation, as I see Cone set down in the plain language of incredulity that white women and children were invited to be the first to cull body parts or bits of clothing from the living victim hanging from the tree; that lynchings were family outings; that photographers flocked to them; that the photos remained in family albums; that this was happening in the 1950s, the age we are encouraged to think of in a soap-sud lather of the re-emergence of housewifery and a new world order. Yes, I knew that this had been happening; I did not know that we, that writers, were allowed. Does this mean that 'memory studies', 'the photograph', 'transgenerational trauma' and 'disenfranchisement' can be openly rethought? Must be? By everyone? May I talk about this in the university? At festivals? I know I can talk about it to the community who let me recover in their poustinia. They know the bony facts.

Coincidence / *hazard*

ROBYN MARSACK

The notion of *hasard objectif* is one of the central tenets of Surrealism as conceived by André Breton. It concerns disturbing coincidences, lacking all logic or reason, fathomed not merely subjectively but by some verifiable, external evidence. Photographs, for instance, as in his novel *Nadja*. I can't really claim that my research into the history of my paternal grandparents meets this definition, but it is marked by unexpected coincidences. My friend D says that because of this new focus, I'm more attuned or receptive to certain things that were already out there, unnoticed. Like filings to a magnet, I say.

Reading through the letters my grandfather Charles Marsack sent to his old friend David Mansfield, whose widow must have given them to my mother, I found an account of an outing in Samoa. Charles was then Chief Justice of the territory. On 29 September 1952 he wrote:

> The producer [i.e. Director] is pleased with the picture 'Return to Paradise' and predicts a substantial box-office success. Len Sinclair, Chérie [my grandmother] and I drove out to Lefaga one Saturday to see the company at work. Very dull, really; they go over and over a scene lasting perhaps a minute until you are sick of the sight and sound of it. The producer pulls no punches with his criticisms. He made the leading lady, Roberta Haynes, do one entrance about twenty times and was still dissatisfied; so he called her over and said 'For heaven's sake, Roberta, try to walk like a human being.' Gary Cooper has to carry a sewing-machine into the fale [house/hut]. After he had done this thirty times he told me that he had never realised how heavy a thing like a sewing-machine can get. They had to wipe the sweat off his brow each time before the camera started turning. Raymond [my uncle] had a walk-on part – as a British officer – in the Apia sequence. In the cabaret scene he blew smoke-rings at the camera and Mark Robson the producer thought it was a good idea. I had several long yarns with Gary Cooper, who is a quiet well-spoken fellow with none of the boastfulness and self-importance we are led to expect in screen stars. Roberta roamed about Apia in a blouse and tight-fitting pedal-pushers and a complete lack of glamour. The Samoan girls were attractive in comparison. They at least looked as though they had had a bath.

Something stirred in my mind: I'd read a Samoan view of this film somewhere… Yes, there are two poems about the film in Tusiata Avia's acclaimed first collection, *Wild Dogs under My Skirt* (2004), and one about its aftermath: an abandoned, illegitimate baby. In 'Return to Paradise' she writes about her mixed-race uncle, who was Gary Cooper's body-double:

> He'd studied in Fiji and could speak English
>
> but no one needed him to talk
> he was afakasi
> and white enough to look white.
>
> Cooper didn't come out much in the day
> too hot maybe
> they shot him mostly at night
>
> so my uncle stood in the sun for the long shots
> in those beachcomber shorts and the hat.
> What the villagers remember is the church
>
> where Gary Cooper shoots out the stained glass
> windows with a gun.
> and the machine that pumped water out of the sea

to make it rain.
The boys remember the cigarettes
and the candy that the crew handed out

all through the night so they would stay
and keep them company.

Bracketing these stanzas, Avia recounts an episode of casual violence that her uncle visited on one of the Australian crewmen. In 'Frame', she has obtained a DVD of the film, and can freeze-frame on her relations, extras in the film, including her own father and 'Tupe / the district nurse'. They 'were fleeing' because of a curfew, her father thought; Avia sees that it is a moment of revolt by the villagers against missionary puritanism: 'he doesn't know / about the revolution / he thinks it was a fiafia' [celebration]. So the film for her is necessarily complicated: it provides employment and amusement; it takes what it wants from the island without regard for the consequences. The sweating Gary Cooper described by my grandfather is replaced by Avia's uncle when the American can't stand the heat. Avia's was a breakthrough volume for Pacific poets, revolutionary – even in the small matter of not italicising Samoan words – and celebratory, speaking out defiantly for young women.

I mentioned this coincidence of experiences when visiting my cousin Laurette, the keeper of the Marsack archive. She said, 'Oh yes, Mum told me that Dad taught Gary Cooper how to blow smoke rings'. She rustled through a box of her family photos, and came up with one that Auntie Betty had taken on set: 'She had to crawl under a chair to get this, she wasn't supposed to be there'. It's not a flattering photograph of Cooper. In his pristine white T-shirt, he sits at a table in the fale, a large bunch of bananas hanging over the doorway, his hand out to catch the rain dripping through a hole in the roof. 'Taken from 10 feet away', Auntie Betty has written on the back. My Scottish family can scarcely believe all this.

I don't have the same degree of passion and knowledge about films as they have. And I don't share S's fascination with Surrealism. Yet here I am, trying to trace the history of my grandparents' meeting in France, he serving in the New Zealand army in the First World War, and she... well one thing I now know for sure, which none of us knew when she was alive, is that she had a relationship with André Breton. They were both very young when they met in Nantes in 1916.

*

Before we visited Nantes, S thought to show me Agnes Varda's lovely film about the childhood and adolescence of her husband Jacques Demy, *Jacquot de Nantes* (1991). His father was the owner of a garage and a car-repair business in Nantes, during the period of the Occupation; Jacques, from a very young age, was a cinephile, enchanted with the whole process of movie making. We see him persuading his mother that he needs a second-hand camera he has glimpsed in the window of a shop in the Passage Pommeraye, a nineteenth-century shopping arcade beloved of the Surrealists and featured in several of Demy's films.

In Demy's *Lola*, the protagonist Michel returns to Nantes after spending many years in the South Pacific. Lola, a night-club singer and dancer, is the mother of his son from their earlier love affair. While waiting for his return, she has taken up with an American sailor, but she is also loved by a boyfriend from her adolescence, Roland Cassard. Cassard resigns from his office job and takes off for the cinema. It wasn't until I was reading Bill Marshall's evocative essay 'Passages of Nantes' that I registered what film Cassard went to see: *Return to Paradise*, 'in which an ex-serviceman [Cooper] goes back to a lost love on a Samoan island (Matareva, where Michel has spent many of his lost years)', Marshall explains. He sees Demy's film in the context of France at the time: living 'the twin upheavals of economic transformation and decolonisation [...] haunted by the "Americanising" implied in these processes'. That seems equally applicable to New Zealand and Samoa, if on a smaller scale.

Lola was released in 1961, the year before Samoa gained independence from New Zealand, and my grandparents moved to Fiji, making a new home for themselves – five years before Tusiata Avia was born. These are stories of colonised and colonisers, of migrations, questions of where people feel 'at home'; my grandmother often going to Tahiti – part of French Polynesia still – to 'top-up her French' as my cousin put it. I'm both alert to and at sea in these coincidences.

In Nantes we go to the Parc de Procé, with its plaque quoting Breton's affectionate tribute to the place, and as in 1916, when my grandmother recited Rimbaud to a French soldier walking there (Breton, it turned out), it happens to be raining.

Notes:
Avia, Tusiata, *Wild Dogs under My Skirt* (Wellington: Victoria University Press, 2004)
Marshall, Bill, *The French Atlantic: Travels in Culture and History* (Liverpool University Press, 2009)

Set 10: Mondon de Ekstera Spaco

TRANSLATED BY JOHN GALLAS

1
While walking
                Edith Södergran (1892–1923)/Sweden

While walking
I passed about the solar systems
until I found the first thread of my red dress.
I know myself well enough by now.
My heart hangs somewhere in space,
streaming sparks, thuddering in the air,
open to another worldless heart.

2
Wang Tu (Tao Chengdao) His Rocket
                Anonymous (poss. fourteenth century)/China

Wang Tu, Imperishable Fan
of all the Technological Advances known to man –
viz. Fireworks, Gunpowder, Rockets, Lift, Thrust and the Stars –
built a bamboo chair (+ kite) in which to journey to Mars.
On liftoff day, clad in a gold-and-silk-thread *páo,*
he sat himself down, with a *yi lu ping an* bow,
and asked his forty-seven servants to light
the forty-seven rockets tied to his chair and kite.
There followed a great explosion. Bang. When the smoke cleared
Wang Tu and his Shénzhōu had disappeared.

It is certain Wang Tu is now sailing happily through Outer Space.
Our Astronomers have recently observed his face.

páo: a long, one-piece robe
yi lu ping an: may your voyage be safe and peaceful
Shénzhōu: Divine Vessel on the Heavenly River – the name of several Chinese spacecraft

3
Goodbye to a Spaceman
                Ojārs Vācietis (1933–1983)/Latvia

It's me, child: your planet, Earth.
I can't promise my radiowaves
will get to you everytime and everywhere.
I can't promise that my rocketsteel will last.
But you will, because you are my child:
and when that faith fails, it fails in my own grey
   crowns and clouds.

When a train leaves I am indifferent.
When a ship leaves I feel very little.
But when your rocket fires… my childlove will blaze.
I am your mother. Nothing can tear you from my arms.

My love will not loose you, my gravity-grip
will drag you back with dear greed. *Don't go!*
Don't listen. *Come back quickly.* Come back.

Come back quickly, with starflakes on your boots.
Come back quickly, with stars ablink in your eyes.
Come back quickly, with twinkling nerves in your heart.

Along the banks of my creeks my pathways splash,
my bright rain pours down, and my lilacs
will unloose their sweet smell, breezed with stormfresh ozone,
like your lover's spread hair.

It's me, child: your planet, Earth – take from me
on your starry course a ryeloaf, and a clod.

4
Song for Edward Makuka Nkoloso
                Sepo Kamara (twenty-first century)/Zambia

My Space Cadets wear green satin jackets with yellow pants.
They have been trained in flying oildrums, and can walk on their hands.
This is the way they walk in space.

Matha Mwamba will go to Mars, with two cats and a Missionary.
They will proceed afterwards to the moon. My dog, Cyclops,
will join them at a later date. We are called Afronauts.

5
'My wide eyes watch …'
            Anon: Song Text (twentieth century)/Eritrea

My wide eyes watch the hollow sky
through my gap-split, soot-smut roof.
I am a line on my bed, fishing for sleep,
straw-prickled, chaff-stunk.
I hold my careful tears and worldache in,
shut in my swollen eyes.
My wide eyes watch the cold dreaming moon
easy on its star-straw, air-squabbed couch.
I am only pain. My eyes sleep,
but my gap-split heart is wide awake.

Notes:
1. Edith Södergran – from '52 Euros'. Slightly revised.
2. Wang Tu – new.
3. Goodbye to a Spaceman – from 'The Song Atlas'. Relined.
4. Song for Edward Makuka Nkoloso – with kind permission of, and help from, the poet/new.
5. 'My wide eyes watch…' – from 'The Song Atlas'. Relined.

San Luigi

HAL COASE

We had met once before, although that morning I struggled to remember when. A mutual friend had put us in touch. You were staying for a few weeks in one of the backstreets behind Campo de' Fiori. I suggested we meet under Giordano Bruno in the piazza, one Tuesday morning, and then take a walk up towards the river.

'I'm sorry for my hearing', you said the moment we met. 'And I hate English', you added quickly, and then you lifted both your hands inside your jacket pockets so as to say: and that's that.

'You hate English?'

'The language. Yes.'

'OK.'

You switched to French, which I could understand but hardly speak, in order to explain that you had lost all hearing in your left ear and that your right ear 'tired fast': 'So I prefer to walk in silence. If you have something to say, we will stop.'

With this rule established, we could start walking in silence. It was late March and there had been heavy rain through the night, which meant the sharp smells of the flower market mixed with the damp of brown puddles sprung up around street corners. The air felt heavy. On Vittorio Emanuele, the sun cut through behind us and we followed our shadows up towards the river. I filled the silence with questions that I could have asked you, but no question seemed worth stopping us for. I had read a poem of yours last night, translated from the Polish into Italian, and I turned the opening lines over in my head:

Nella casa che vorrei chiamare lingua
ci sono molte stanze.

In the house which I would like to call language
there are many rooms.

Our reticence might've been uncomfortable, only it was ours – and as a gentle proof of this, you turned every now and then to smile at me. Despite this reassurance, I felt, as I often did in those years, that no amount of any language would be of use. I wanted to ask about your poetry and your migrations, about Warsaw in the sixties and Paris in the seventies, your time in Venice and then Rome, about the moves from east to west to east – Polish to French, and then back again. But these curiosities were less urgent than the shared pace we had established, which overlayed my muddle of half-translated thoughts with the rhythm of the street. What I had read of you became subordinated to this rhythm; the foundations over which we now walked.

We had stopped at the river. The month's rainfall had left it swollen and disturbed in its passage between the travertine levees. Where the lower bank opposite had burst, two unfortunate cyclists were pushing their bikes through the river's new edge.

'I don't like cities that bury their rivers', you said, in Italian.

'Isn't that what the majority of cities do?' I replied, in Italian, which meant that the phrase seemed to me stretched somehow.

'*C'est ça* – I don't like the majority of cities.'

In the house which I would like to call language
there are many rooms.
Each of the rooms is older than the house.
They were lived in before
the house was one house.

We decided to walk to San Luigi, which you explained you would visit every morning during your previous stay in the city, when you had lived on Vicolo del Fico. 'Now it is impossible', you said loudly in English, for the benefit of the American students who had suddenly separated us while they joked about one of their friends who was lagging further behind. I couldn't tell exactly what they were laughing at, or I didn't want to understand: English could come to seem distant and yet ferocious to me in these moments, like words spoken in a bad dream.

In the house which I would like to call language
there are many rooms.
Each of the rooms is older than the house.
They were lived in before
the house was one house.
Your visitors alone will know the way: they will climb
The stairs, they will open the doors,

The Contarelli chapel is set to the left of the church's apse. Its dedication to the life of Saint Matthew was ordered in the will of the French cardinal Matthieu Cointerel, following his death in 1585. Giuseppe Cesari finished the frescoes of the vault by 1593. In the central section, Saint Matthew has arrived for the miracle of Ephigenia's resurrection. A shaft of light enters from the right of the scene to illuminate the figures crouched around the bed chamber. The miracle has already occurred, the light merely confirms this.

In the summer of 1599, the commission for the altar decorations would pass to Caravaggio, then a student of Cesari. The little light that arrives from the chapel's south-facing oval window is amplified in the left panel, the Calling of Saint Matthew. It is a light that now changes, miraculously, everything it touches: the worried cheeks; the sack of coins and the boat-like form of an inkwell; the tensed thigh of the man who is just now turning, on the edge of his seat, ready to be counted, or to leave.

In the right panel of the martyrdom, light is suddenly accusatory, incriminating, and yet also complicit in the crime: the body of the Saint's assassin seems powered by the light that the figures to his left leap away from. The violence of this light is also miraculous: its detonation not only what allows us to see, but also what makes of the act of looking a decision and then a commitment, when we might otherwise wish to look away.

> In the house which I would like to call language
> there are many rooms.
> Each of the rooms is older than the house.
> They were lived in before
> the house was any house.
> Your visitors alone will know the way: they will climb
> The stairs, they will open the doors.
> Tomorrow, the house will be theirs,

Positioned as it is directly under the chapel's only window, the altar is a gloomy spot. It must have been the difficulty of handling light in the central panel, you suggested, that made its completion more protracted.

The first version produced by Caravaggio was destroyed in a fire in Berlin in 1945. Black-and-white photos of the work leave a perhaps exaggerated impression of how light worked in the original: the white flare of the angel's wing is balanced by the fleshy white of Matthew's left thigh, thrust forward as though preparing for a step out of the frame. Matthew is writing his testimony, but his entire body is struggling to keep the white of the page centred and still.

The second version reverses this momentum: Matthew has rushed up to his desk; the precarity of his pose suggests fluster and readiness, rather than unease or testiness. If he were to move any further, he would dive into the book open in front of him. Above, the angel is wrapped up in brain-like coils of heavy cloth.

'The angel counts', you said. 'What is he counting?'

'He's putting memory in order? That's inspiration.'

'A translation – you see that the angel's right hand is held like his, but in reverse: they mirror each other.' The strange thing, you went on, is that the book itself is subordinated here. Writing will be the record of whatever language moves between this pair, but that language is first inscribed in the body, which has its own force and gestures, its own grammar.

The light in the chapel went out. We had been standing beside a pillar to the left, among a group of German tourists who had arrived at the same time, and now it was all dark. A huddle formed around the little machine fixed next to the other pillar and we heard the clinking of small change. The light costs fifty cents for one minute or one euro for three minutes. The machine doesn't give change.

> In the house which I would like to call language
> there are many rooms.
> Each of the rooms is older than the house.
> They were lived in before
> the house was any house.
> Your visitors alone will know the way: they will climb
> the stairs, they will open the doors.
> Tomorrow, the house will be theirs,
> just as it was yours, for a time.

Light, again. Its sudden impact on the paintings cued a chorus of hushed amazements in a dozen languages. Then, somewhere in between that noise and the silence of painting, I remembered where it was that I had met you.

Letter from Wales

SAM ADAMS

The Spring 2025 number of *Poetry Wales* celebrates the magazine's sixtieth birthday. To mark the occasion, it features contributions from sixty new poets and reviews by writers who have connections with the magazine extending back almost as far as its now distant origins.

A long time ago the founder and first editor, Meic Stephens, gave me copies of the earliest issues from his personal collection. The title page of 'Number One – Spring 1965' carries the information that it is 'published twice a year by THE TRISKEL PRESS at Garth Newydd, Merthyr Tydfil, in Glamorgan'. At that point the magazine had only eighteen pages and the 'Press' was an imaginary construct. In 1962, newly graduated in French at UCW Aberystwyth, Meic had found a teaching post at the grammar school in Ebbw Vale, a forbidding twenty-two miles uphill from his Taff-side home in Trefforest, near Pontypridd. He was already a Plaid Cymru activist, and that may well have encouraged him to join a small group with similar political engagement living at the Merthyr property, not to mention halving the distance to work. 'Radio Free Wales' briefly broadcast from the attic to a couple of neighbouring streets. Rumoured to have been built for an industrialist, Garth Newydd may have been neglected and run down, but it was a spacious three-storey building for like-minded occupants and, conveniently (remarkably!), had no known owner. Just in case, they put aside a weekly sum for rent, which was never collected.

So *Poetry Wales* (the title inspired by *Poetry Ireland*) began, in the month of May, with no subsidy, no moneyed backer. The bill for printing five hundred copies was forty-seven pounds. As for distribution, Meic sold copies himself and through friends in Plaid Cymru. Quite how he gathered contributors (sixteen of them, including the editor) for that first number I cannot say, but the list included Alison Bielski, Roland Mathias and Harri Webb, who became significant figures in what he subsequently termed 'the second flowering' of Welsh writing in English (the 'first flowering' having been in the 1930s). It concludes with an obituary by Gwyn Jones, Professor of English, for T. Harri Jones, not long before a student in his department at Aberystwyth. This farmer's boy from the rural heart of Wales near Builth Wells, and poet of huge promise, had recently been appointed to a lectureship in English on the other side of the world, at the University of New South Wales, but had hardly established himself there when he drowned in a sea-fed swimming pool. The second number, 'Autumn 1965', is more sure of itself. It has book reviews, includes probably the most memorable of the editor's own poems, 'Ponies, Twynyrodyn' and, although a note on the title page reiterates, with regret, a warning to contributors that 'no payment can be made', it has poems from Dannie Abse, Anthony Conran, Leslie Norris and Sally Roberts (Jones).

In Meic's correspondence, and soon in conversation, the new project was *PW* and the abbreviation stuck. Publication three times a year began in Spring 1966, but there was still no money to pay contributors. That did not dismay Raymond Garlick, Leslie Norris and John Tripp, a trio whose long connection with the magazine began with that number, nor indeed Bobi Jones, who had the distinction of being the magazine's first Welsh-language poet. From that point on, there were always poems in the senior language of Wales. A brief hiatus in Meic's editorship (1967–8) coincided with the commencement of his appointment as Literature Officer (subsequently Literature Director) at the Welsh Arts Council. Gwilym Rees Hughes became Welsh editor at this juncture and continued in the role when Meic returned. This was, for me, a stroke of fortune indeed, because Gwilym and I were colleagues at the time and, with the magazine now increased in scope and size, and published quarterly, he introduced me to Meic as someone who might look after reviews. Meic and I had a good deal in common. Notably, this was a Glamorgan upbringing and student experience at Aberystwyth: we had both in our time edited the college magazine. And some years later I briefly succeeded Meic as editor of *PW* until a job change took me away.

Garth Newydd was demolished in the 1970s. Professor Meic Stephens died in July 2018. *Poetry Wales* has had a number of editors over its sixty years – from memory I recall Cary Archard, Richard Poole, Mike Jenkins and Robert Minhinnick. Currently the chair is occupied by Zoë Skoulding.

FROM THE ARCHIVE

Marina Tsvetaeva's 'New Year's Greetings'

Elaine Feinstein

Happy New Year – new sphere – horizon – haven!
This is my first letter to your new address,
– notorious region, misunderstood, unsettled –,
as clamorous and empty as the Aeolian tower;
my very first letter to you from the yesterday
in which I suddenly found myself without you,
my own homeland become one of the stars....
Shall I tell you how I heard the news?

[...]

from PNR 184, vol. 35, no. 2
November – December 2008

Contributors to the issue included
Frank Kuppner, Robert Saxton,
Eavan Boland and Vénus Khoury-Ghata

For more from the archive visit
www.pnreview.co.uk

PNR

Features

The Library as Macrocosm and Microcosm

The closing lecture at the Bibliothèque de France in Paris to celebrate its thirtieth anniversary

ALBERTO MANGUEL

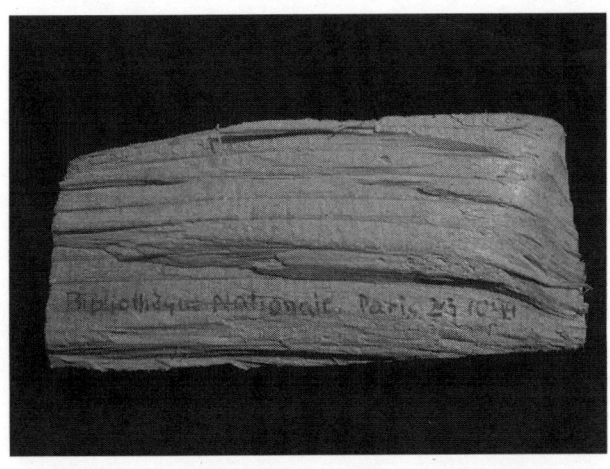

On 23 October 1994, I decided to visit the much-vaunted site in Bercy where the new national library of France was going to be built. Much earlier, when I was in my twenties, I had gone to read in the old library, the one on the Rue Richelieu, to research for the *Dictionary of Imaginary Places* that I was writing with my friend, Gianni Guadalupi. And because that was the first national library of France I knew, for me, that noble building and its stately Salle Labrouste were (perhaps in my mind still are) an indelible monument in my private French geography. First loves are often the ones that remain steadfast and are blind to factual reason.

National libraries, whether almost mythical ones such as that of Alexandria, or almost too down-to-earth ones such as the Vernadsky National Library of Ukraine, are above all symbolic buildings. They incarnate the identity of their readers, be they ambitious kings or resilient victims, reflecting back to them what these men and women, as readers, have understood to be their cultural and political memory, their language and their literature, the evidence of their existence and the inspiration of their mythologies. Ordinary libraries, whether private or public, are worlds defined by their chosen contents and their selective use. A national library, however, is the vaster universe that echoes and preserves them. A private library is an autobiography told in the voice of its reader, but a national library is the collective answer to the curse of Babel, alchemically transforming the linguistic chaos with which God intended to punish human ambition into a generous and intelligent ordering of things. Also, and this of the essence, into an instrument for dialogue and understanding.

On that day in Bercy three decades ago, walking along the edge of the great gaping hole from which the new BnF would rise, I picked up a small piece of wood dropped by one of the workers, wrote the date on it and kept it on my desk, because I superstitiously believe that colossal things such as the new BnF, things that are perhaps too big to be seen properly, require a metaphor or an emblem that you can hold in your hand to come to terms with their grandeur: a microcosm, as it were, that implies in its smallness the macrocosm that contains it.

The Greek Stoics, and later the Talmudic commentators, considered the universe to be a living creature made up of a body and a soul. Consequently, if the universe is an exaggerated version of a human being, then a human being is a reduced version of the ineffable universe. The Stoics and the Talmudists believed that the human soul, as part of the universal soul, is to the human body what the universal soul is to the universe, and that the rational part of that soul works within each of us just like the universal intellect works in the whole of the universe. Most importantly, they also believed that the macrocosm influences the microcosm, and vice versa. If the whole universe is one organic body possessing life, motion and a soul, then the library could be considered the repository of both souls – the universal and the human one. That is what Borges meant when he suggested that the terms *universe* and *library* are synonymous.

Libraries are places in which the imagination can feel at home. The library of the Rue Richelieu seemed to me a perfect place to read about Fourier's Phalanstère and Campanella's Città del Sole, Casanova's Protocosmo and Rabelais's Mer de mots gelés. As a reader, I believe that the frame of a text is all-important, because it colours and defines, limits and expands, the words that flow across the page or screen. The Salle Labrouste, occupied today by the Institut national d'histoire de l'art (INHA), contrary to what its external appearance might suggest, is the realisation of that classic impossibility: the squaring of a circle. The Salle Labrouste is a square crowned by nine domes, supported by metal columns in the form of tree trunks. And the repetition of the arches suggests, at least it did to me, that reading is a circular activity, beginning on a page hidden in some volume that I would never open on a shelf that I would never reach, and ending (but there is no end to reading) on another page equally hidden and remote.

Squaring the circle was a problem proposed by Anaxagoras in the fifth century B.C.; in the late nineteenth century, the mathematician Ferdinand von Lindemann definitively proved this to be an impossible task. And yet, the fascination with accomplishing that which is proven impossible stubbornly persists in the human imagination: we are always seeking ways of coining the face of the wind and making a rope of sand. Since the beginning of time, we have believed that one day we will be able to determine the true nature of the unicorn, what song the sirens sang, and the best system of government to render a society a little more just and a little less unhappy. Libraries, in their almost infinite capacity, tempt us with the expectation of finding these solutions in one of their shrouded volumes. The Salle Labrouste was, and perhaps still is, in spite of the proof to the contrary, a successful and fruitful squaring of the circle.

The present BnF too is a squared circle, the square being in this case the book-shaped towers of glass now lined with wood, sitting on its vast mastaba, and the circle the all-encompassing realm of human knowledge contained within its bowels. Like the wishful collection in the Mouseion of the Ptolemian kings, the BnF is a macrocosm that has everything, or close to everything – but it is at the same time a microsom of our experience. One example: in December 1996, the BnF opened an exhibition called 'Tous les savoirs du monde' to celebrate the inauguration of the new site. The show traced six millennia of encyclopedias, displaying numerous examples of our passion for classifying our knowledge and for making lists, from fragments of the earliest repertoires inscribed in cuneiform script on Sumerian clay tablets, to one of the 10,040 chapters of the *Grande encyclopédie impériale illustrée des temps passé et présent* of Chen Menglei, of 1726, an oriental contemporary of the better-known *Encyclopédie, ou dictionnaire raisonné des sciences, des arts et des métiers* of Diderot and D'Alembert – all presented to the curious public in the BnF's brand-new display cases. Perhaps the notion of an encyclopedia belongs to the collective imagination. In the nineteen-sixties, the mathematician Roger Penrose suddenly came to the realisation that every particle, every force, every light cone, every cause, effect, law and property, might be, in its most fundamental form, a pure, glorious, complex geometry, forming a new and stunning picture of reality. A library such as the new BnF can be understood to be the universal representation of such comprehensive geometry.

In the thirty years since my first encounter with the ambitious foundations of the BnF, much has changed in the world of libraries. The census of 2023 showed that the BnF held over 16 million printed books, more than 400,000 periodicals, close to 400,000 manuscripts, and over 16 million images. To these were added over 54,000 million web archives. Today, of course, these figures have increased. This impressive number, fruit of our electronic age, carries with it a new danger. The Library of Alexandria was threatened by fire, water, looters, bookworms and other noxious creatures. The BnF, whose holdings are in their vast majority virtual, is today threatened not only by cyberpirates, like the ones who attacked the British Library in October 2023, whose electronic holdings have not yet been fully restored, but also by the possibility of rendering intellectual research and creativity obsolete. The electronic technology has enriched us, but also rendered us more vulnerable. The making of the waters on the Second Day of Creation carried within it the threat of the future Universal Deluge. The making of the so-called Artificial Intelligence carries within it the temptation of relinquishing our humanity to statistical machines.

In a text composed in its original Semitic version in the first century and later included in the Apocrypha, known as the *Life of Adam and Eve,* Eve asks her son Seth to write her story and that of his father Adam. At the end of the book, in a meta-literary flourish, Eve says to him: 'Listen to me, my child! Make tablets of stone and others of clay, and write on them all my life and your father's and all that you have heard and seen from us. If the Lord judge our race by water, the tables of clay will be dissolved and the tables of stone will remain; but if by fire, the tables of stone will be broken up and the tables of clay will be baked hard'. Every text depends for its survival and its reading, as we have noted, on its framework, but also on the qualities of its support, be it clay or stone, paper or screen. No text is ever exclusively analogue or virtual, independent of its material context: every text is defined by both its words and by the space in which those words exist. No doubt the BnF is conscious of this, and in these days when intellect and creativity, memory and reason, are once again threatened, it may be useful to remind ourselves of the fragility of our libraries of clay and paper and virtual texts.

I said that a national library symbolically incarnates the identity of its readers. This means not only who these readers believe themselves to be, but also what they choose to forget of their past experience. Because, as the director of the Bodleian Library, Richard Ovenden, has said, a library is a place of evidence: it shows not only our documented reality, but also what we choose not to remember, what we would rather forget or ignore. All libraries exist under the shadow of censorship, whether from deliberate exclusion or from necessity, whether from a government's fears or from physical lack of space and funds. And yet, even when censored, a national library serves as a reminder of what we may generously aspire to in the best of all possible worlds, or what we may regret losing.

Since the beginning of time, we have known that, as individuals of a species, we cannot survive alone. However, also as individual of the species, we are constantly tempted to relinquish that which brings us together and helps us endure the threats that surround us. We are all of us granted the possibility of possessing faith, hope and charity – above all *caritas*, without which all other powers are nothing. As is proven again and again, and in spite of the loud proclamations of bloodthirsty tyrants and *la droite decomplexée*, selfishness is not a virtue, and if a person chooses to benefit himself alone at the expense of all others, that person is condemning himself to suicide. A library holds on its shelves both options, the first under the label of the ecumenical discovery of Rimbaud, that *Je est un autre*; the second under the stupefying cry of fascist Spain, *Viva la muerte*.

In his 2009 book *The Master and His Emissary*, the psychiatrist Iain McGilchrist argued that the two hemispheres of the human brain can be seen as respectively logical and creative, the left hemisphere being detail-oriented, the right being whole-oriented. These two modes of perception are not exclusive, they simply prioritize one capacity over the other. The right hemisphere oversees our surroundings, the general view, looking out for the consequences of our actions. The left hemisphere concentrates on picking out a single prey, the object of our intentions. Left to its own devices, a society privileging the left hemisphere will tend to forgo empathy, neglect the environment, become blind to the results of egotistical actions centred in the present moment. A Talmudist might see the left hemisphere as the microcosm, and the right hemisphere as the macrocosm: the conflictive relationships of both parings, the biological and the mystical, are similar. Our histories seem to indicate that, since the time of the Industrial Revolution at least, the left hemisphere has come to dominate our societies, and that we have closed ourselves in our single shells from our fellow human beings and the world at large. Our libraries, however, continue to insist that both hemispheres are of the essence. Whether we pay attention to the evidence is another matter.

In ancient Sumeria, events in earthly politics and religion were seen as parallels of heavenly ones: events on earth are reflected, and have to be explained, by events in heaven. The conduct of a king, for instance, was mirrored in the conduct of heavenly bodies, and the secret ways of the gods were revealed in the entrails of a sacrificial animal. In one of the oldest epics that has come down to us, it is told that the people of the City of Uruk lived under the despotic rule of a cruel young king called Gilgamesh whose laws were unjust and whose pleasure lay in their pain. King Gilgamesh cast aside intellectual pursuits. He enjoyed wrestling and making other men wrestle with him, 'even when they had better things to do', and he liked to have his way with young women, and also with brides-to-be. The people of Uruk were understandably unhappy and prayed to the gods to find a way to make things better. They did not pray for the death of Gilamesh, because they knew that a society must find ways to heal itself without resorting to murder. To remedy the situation, the gods sent a wild man, Enkidu, to wrestle with the king, and in the bodily struggle between corrupt civilisation and innocent nature both men emerged as better people. Throughout our histories, under other names, Gilgamesh must learn to be a better ruler and Enkidu must acquire the civilised laws of society, over and over again. Human societies must be based on certain common rules, as well as laws of justice and *caritas,* and we have to keep repeating them in order not to lose our bearings in the path of what we like to think of as progress. 'Clearly,' wrote G. K. Chesterton, 'there could be no safety for a society in which the remark by the Chief Justice that murder was wrong was regarded as an original and dazzling epigram.' In order for society to protect itself from itself, these truisms need to be posted above every door and displayed on every mantlepiece.

There never seems to be a definitive conclusion to our trials and errors. The human microcosm returns again and again to a state of wilful injustice and selfish ambition, concentrating on what one individual wants for himself alone, and again and again the macrocosm must mirror back the consequences of these actions in an attempt to restore the balance, especially now, in this world that seems to have grown suddenly so murky. But as Juan Gabriel Vásquez has so wisely said, 'we are very bad judges of the present moment, perhaps because the present does not really exist: everything is memory, and this sentence that I have just written is already a memory'. In the case of Gilgamesh, this occurs with the death of his beloved Enkidu, the incarnation of Nature; in our case, with warnings of the foreseeable extinction of human life on earth. Gilgamesh's subjects prayed to the gods for salvation; perhaps for us, more effective than prayers, are small, persistent and stubborn acts of resistance.

Small acts of resistance that don't allow willed catastrophes to happen in silence, small refusals to acquiesce on unjust occasions, small withdrawals of collaboration in deeds of wilful destruction: these are some of the strategies that might perhaps allow for our survival. In Jewish tradition, human salvation depends on thirty-six just men known as the *Lamed-vovniks*, good men who are not aware of the existence of one another, and on whom rests the fate of the world. Islam increases this figure by four. Caliph Uthman ibn Affan, companion of the Prophet, heard his father say that the number of the just are forty. 'Forty men?' asked Caliph Uthman. 'Don't say men', his father answered. 'Rather say humans, because there are women among them.' The least visible of us can be one of the *Lamed-vovniks*, but to recognize him or her we need *caritas*, the power of empathy.

The literature that we have collected over the ages on the shelves of our libraries, in its rich and endless ambiguity, can teach us empathy with Shylock but also with Macbeth, pity for Priam but also for Achilles, love for Antigone but also for Hecuba, sympathy for Madame

Bovary but also for her more discreet husband. It can show us that, as is told in the *Odyssey*, every life is a voyage, and, as is told in the *Iliad*, every life is a battle, and that we are all exiles and toilers. It allows us, like Bartleby, to refuse to become the accomplice of senseless bureaucracy and unjust systems, and gives us permission to say out loud 'I would prefer not to'. Unfortunately, today's rhetoric is the contrary of literature. It has no ambiguity, no open questions to incite dialogue. It propounds the contrary of *caritas*: the unimportance of the other, or worse, the other's inexistence. It echoes Rome's *Cartago delenda est*. It commits genocide, it razes cultures considered alien, it imprisons artists and writers, and burns books.

As any reader must know, this state of affairs is not unique to our time. In 213 B.C., the Chinese Emperor Qin Shi Huang condemned to the flames the works of Confucius and had 460 Confucian scholars burnt alive. In 1258, the Mongol Prince Hulegu Khan set fire to the Library or House of Wisdom during the siege of Baghdad. In 1562, the Catholic bishop Diego de Landa ordered the destruction of the Maya codices of Yucatán. In nineteenth-century New York, Anthony Comstock, founder in 1873 of the Society for the Suppression of Vice, destroyed some fifteen tons of books he considered objectionable. In 1933, the Nazis assembled truckloads of so called 'un-German' books and threw them into the bonfire at Bebelplatz in Berlin. In our century, too, there is no dearth of examples.

In February 2025, Israeli police raided the Educational Bookshop in East Jerusalem, a place of dialogue between Israelis and Palestinians, frequented by foreign diplomats, visiting writers and everyday readers. Two booksellers, Mahmood Muna and Ahmed Muna, were detained on house arrest and forbidden to return to their *librarie* for fifteen days. The French language has happily made *librarie* and *bibliothèque* synonymous. As you know, the BnF was born as the Librarie du Roi, set up in 1368 in the Louvre Palace by Charles V and consisting of 917 manuscripts catalogued by the first royal librarian, Gilles Maillard. Whether *librarie* or *bibliothèque*, the assault on a site that holds books is a crime against humanity, and can be added to the vast and sorry list of violence against the word.

However, these acts do not happen in the shadows. There are always witnesses to these acts, and eventually recording angels will appear to attest to these infamies. A voice that makes itself heard, a private legal denunciation, a grassroots protest set up to oppose the crime, a courageous solitary sign held up silently – all of these show that the microcosm too can influence the workings of the overwhelming macrocosm.

As in the case of the *Lamed-vovniks*, we may never know the name, religion or nationality of this one woman demonstrating at the site of the raided bookstore in Jerusalem, but the image of her presence is enough to show that resistance, however minuscule, is always an option when facing injustice. This image of the protester is of crucial importance, and it should be displayed here, at the BnF, in this universe that contains '*tous les savoirs du monde*', for all readers to see it and to find in it hope.

Because, superstitiously, I believe that small things, such as a single person standing up against tyranny, can become a symbol, a metaphor, an emblem raised high against that vast wave of destruction falling over the world once again today. We must remember that the left hemisphere of our brain can make us concentrate, not only on selfishly procuring our prey, but also on identifying flaws in the societal model that our selfishness has created. And in doing so, it can help the macrocosm, infected as it is by never-ending greed and blind violence, to heal itself once more and to provide a healthier frame for our life on earth. Like an illuminating word in a book waiting patiently to be opened by its intended reader, this image unerringly shows us the power of the imaginative microcosm mirroring the imagined wished-for macrocosm wherein it is contained.

Poems

IRYNA SHUVALOVA

Translated by Uilleam Blacker

(The poem below was written in response to the death, in a Russian air strike, of the Ukrainian writer Victoria Amelina)

I sit here like a dog and don't understand death
I don't get it I don't follow
I can't get my head around it
with my dog's brains
here is a person

and now only her clothes remain her boots
the left sole slightly more worn on the inside
the torn edge of the coat pocket sewn up
by a hand that
suddenly no longer knows how to sew
or write or hold a knife or fork or stroke
her son's head or click her fingers
impatiently
can we learn all this again somewhere after the end

receipts in a handbag – from the drycleaners the café
some crumbs from a pastry
bought on the way home from work
what are they for, these traces of our presence, if
our absence
will always snap shut behind us
like the doors of the metro train
trapping the edge of our favourite jacket

sometimes we think in grand terms
we look down stunned unblinking
into the black holes now gaping in the body
of our time of our country but I
from the humble height of my dog's muzzle
my dog's heart
can only think one thing:
don't go

brush some more crumbs from the table
water the cactus and swear in a traffic jam
sneeze into your sleeve and screw up your face
at the taste of an unripe apricot
keep loving the winter more than the summer
no need for anything else
no films no paintings no festivals no brilliant novels

to hell with paintings and to hell with novels
just be, somewhere, please

Two poems from the series 'Nanjing poems'
(a series reflecting on the poet's time spent living in China)

Osmanthus

when this city stops smelling of osmanthus
I don't know what it will smell of maybe blood
like in an abattoir or maybe of the stone
in mausoleums where they buried those who smelled of blood
or those whose hands reeked of blood or maybe their mouths

what will this city smell of after the osmanthus maybe iron
of blood-sated knives maybe lead
of bullets trained to swim through meat through blood
like effortless swimmers crossing
night-time lakes or maybe the city will smell
only of night water
life water death water – water where

a salty red drop becomes shapeless
turns into a cloud then smoke and then dissolves
into death water life water night water
water smelling like the autumn in this city of the living
and the dead but mainly
of the dead

autumn in this great red land
on this broad endless street
where the blood-swollen sun
sinks but won't set
where any moment now

the osmanthus
blossom
will wither
the osmanthus

will
wilt

The city of the living and the dead

city of the living and the dead and the birds but mainly of the living
who hurry to close the windows on the upper floors
when the great wind blows from the yangtze the great storm
the great storm from the great river
and we so small
scurrying along the roads in our rattling rides
flashing our terrible knives
to reveal the sweet insides of the bamboo
laughing and showing our big yellow teeth
our tiny white fox teeth
or not showing our teeth at all
spitting our laughter into our hands like an unripe plum

city of the living and the dead and the birds but mainly
of the dead who lie quietly
under the tortoise shells of motorways under the wedding cakes
of high-rises
city of those who toss and turn sleepless at the bottom of lakes in pleasant parks
on the slopes of green hills under picnic duvets
in the scrubland beyond the neighbours' allotments
city of those whose sleepless bones have been trampled by horses on roadsides
of those whose mausoleums puff out their empty chests
and those thrown into pits and ditches cast into the wide yangtze
who cannot sleep or lie still who wander at night peering into windows
who call out the names of distracted passers-by
we must close the shutters carefully turn out the lights
hide quickly under the duvet for who knows what
the great wind will bring us and we so small
the great wind from the great yangtze

city of the living and the dead and the birds but mainly of the birds
that stand guard on one leg each night in the park lakes
that get lost white as they are in the sky white from city lights
the way a lovingly tied thread now loose
slips from a slender wrist

city of those whose names I don't know but to whom I call
in a language that to them is nothing but chirping
just like the speech of my wingless neighbours is to me

city of those who built their nest in the osmanthus by my window
and watch me day after day
so defenceless so merciless
as though asking with their dark eyes
what what

will the great wind
from the great yangtze
bring to us
to us, the small and winged
or us, the wingless and small

Nothing is going to happen to us

alisa have you realised now that no harm will come to us
that nobody will block our way in this dark alley
that there was no need for your mother to spend half the night calling your friends
and we will wake up in the morning alive and well
maybe just a little older a little sadder
unfortunately no wiser
did you know alisa?

alisa it looks as though that shotgun hanging on the wall
will no longer be able to shoot us in the face
it is no longer fitting for us to be startled by the light by too much air let's
    instead be careful square flat as we walk above the thunderous
hell of laughter above the fiery chasm of love
let's breathe evenly hold our backs straight and avoid
looking down

see now I've begun to understand
that others will leave us but that we will stay here alisa
and only the heads of burs we lopped off with our wooden swords
year on year grow back this hundred-headed hydra of life
laughs with its flowering jaws in the face of
pale, wretched death
maybe it's not true that death always has the last laugh alisa

remember
how we would open the door and each time
find ourselves in new rooms full of doors we are still
choosing we still have options but
fewer and fewer alisa if only someone had told us
how loudly and irrevocably those doors slam shut behind us
that is the sound of our dead applauding
congratulating us on our flowering wilting rotting
and flowering again

they say that time is an infernal machine alisa but no
time is a black cabriolet with an open top
it is a carriage full of gypsies and bears
it is a hearse that carries the fiddlers to the wedding
it creaks and rocks with the music
and when it finally runs over us alisa
such rampant red roses
will burst from our ridiculous
already useless
bodies

Benjamin in Moscow

SASHA DUGDALE

It's 1926, and the porters of the third-class Moscow Hotel 'Tirol' are sitting in a little room off the lobby, bored to death. Outside the night air is silent and the pavements are treacherous, covered in damp ice. Occasionally a sleigh passes on the ring road, but otherwise sound has been sucked out of the world.

Follow the dimly-lit narrow corridor from the lobby, a threadbare runner tacked to the boards, and it leads to Walter Benjamin's room. There are low voices inside, speaking in German; one reading, another commenting from time to time. The Austrian theatre director, Bernhard Reich, is going through the draft of an article about a landmark Meyerhold production. The stale air of the hotel room, the cigarette smoke, the poor light and the smell of boiling laundry and sweat – it all presses in on his listener and produces a familiar sense of abjection, but also an intoxication with the moment, a strange and foreign moment.

*

Moscow all around him, a low-built bazaar of a place, its deep infrequent church bells rising through the late afternoon. And that very afternoon he had walked under the widest skies, prairie skies; pink, sharp winter air. Moscow: a large plant in its own atmosphere, its shoots struggling to breach the earth and meet the twentieth century.

*

Theatre is a fleeting artform, but Meyerhold's historic 1926 production of Nikolai Gogol's *The Government Inspector* has been well documented in film, articles, memoirs and critical essays. We can never really know what it felt like to be in the audience, and every show would have been different anyway – productions evolve and shift depending on the relationship between audience and cast on any given night. It's only in retrospect that a theatrical event assumes historical importance, only in its surrounding documentation and not in itself. It assumes a defining shape once its vitality is gone and its actors are dispersed. In this it is much like a life.

The action of the play took place on a curved stage with little jutting platforms; a semicircle of polished wood and fifteen opening doors formed the backdrop. The action, compressed into short episodes in this claustrophobic space, had the appearance of a 'moving bouquet' or 'structured kaleidoscope' according to one critic. Unlike Meyerhold's earlier iconic constructivist productions (already in the theatre's museum), the constricted set of *The Government Inspector* was extravagantly furnished: antique bureaux, brocade and crystal, bronze and mahogany. It was an interior with all its signs of life, but no inhabitant: an opened-up and preserved corpse.

*

In 1991 I slept in a large room with a varnished parquet floor, creamy old-fashioned plaster ceiling and some stiff, formal furniture: an armchair, a patterned divan and a large showy desk. An alcove on the right-hand side holds a narrow single bed upholstered in faded damask, covered in cotton sheets and a blanket. A fridge hums in the corner of the room, filled with plastic bags of food. The window behind the desk is typically deep-set, doubled-paned, with only the thinnest curtains clipped to a rod. When the top windows are open for ventilation, the noise outside pours into the room: the rumbling of a tram, the clang of its bells, crows, the dripping of icicles on the building's pediments and sills.

Inside the apartment, voices; shouting from the kitchen, shouting on the telephone in the hall.

A little gold hostess trolley clatters past my door, towers of china cups, wobbling. Bookshelves line the walls of the living room, the odd book pressed flat against the glass like a sign: a glossy album of the Jack of Diamonds artists; another on theatre designs of the twenties; Hemingway in black and white, the Karsh portrait in the fisherman's jumper; Soviet bards on vinyl sleeves.

It's not a preserved corpse, this interior, but a mineral accretion, a geological formation, stopped in its tracks. There is no energy left to adapt to the new chaotic situation: no one even reads a book from cover to cover any more because a storm is blowing in Paradise and Benjamin's Angel of History is being irresistibly propelled into the future.

The kitchen is small and heaped with diaries, glass jars, enamel pans, a little conical vase with a dying rose. The woman whose kitchen this is goes out to work every morning in a woollen suit with an onyx brooch at the throat, but her scientific research and her scavenging for food are interchangeable. There is nothing in the shops and no one would look askance if she left her laboratory to buy or barter something. Sometimes she comes home with a briefcase full of sugar.

In the evening this woman I loved so much perches on a stool, holding a thin piece of bread and butter and an elegant cup of tea, and tells me how she was left on her own in the kitchen of a Moscow communal apartment in the 1940s while her parents were at work. She was so scared of the mice and rats she could hear behind the walls she would sit and drum on a saucepan.

On winter afternoons when she is at work I sit in the kitchen alone, reading the newspaper with a dictionary close by. There is a rubbish chute in the corner with a heavy hopper for a door, and in the silence I hear packets floating down the chute and brushing gently against the walls like wings on their long fall to earth.

*

Meyerhold described his working approach as 'musical realism' in a newspaper interview in November 1926. This musicality is expressed in such gestures as the fifteen polished doors opening simultaneously to reveal townspeople with cash bribes in their hands, or the whole cast moving as one rhythmic whole to the 'Gogolian nerve'. Khlestakov was depicted variously as a chameleon, a devil, an infernal creature, something from Hoffmann.

*

Honesty and the lyric principle are not always aligned. I must keep them both in view as I train my eye to focus on one, and then the other. 'When we speak of honesty, in relation to poems, we mean the degree to which and the power with which the generating impulse has been transcribed', writes Louise Glück, in her essay 'Against Sincerity'. But who knows the generating impulse? It comes from an unseen place and so the degree of transcription is more like a trick of geometry.

*

I recognise in Benjamin an ability to generate the spirit-life, which is something apart and has its own geometry.

*

In August 1991 there was a sudden and defiantly historical event: a putsch. Tanks lined the streets, so for three days we stayed indoors. When it ended we stood around the television in the kitchen and watched the funeral of three men who died in a clash with armed forces. Everyone cried, so I cried too.

What shall I call you, history?

I have no name
I am but two days old –

*

Meyerhold was arrested, tortured, and then executed in 1940 (in the same year that Benjamin took his own life trying to escape from occupied France) and he was only rehabilitated in the fifties, after Stalin's death. Benjamin testifies to the fact that this 1926 production of *The Government Inspector* was not well received: the Party had pronounced against it, the critics weighed in, and Benjamin felt the applause was measured, as if each audience member was calibrating their personal response to the political atmosphere. Meyerhold's indisputable reign was coming slowly to an end, and official approval for this work was subtly withheld.

*

Fragments of the production can be seen online: in one clip a woman, dressed like a doll in full skirts and laced slippers, waves a black feathered fan mechanically. Like all early film it's hard to see in her the real woman who comes off a stage fifty years before I was born and asks another woman in the dressing room to unbutton her corset. Meanwhile the last audience member files out of the auditorium and the house lights are dimmed.

*

During those putsch days, a woman I became friends with much later in my life, and then lost to political persecution, was having an affair in a Moscow apartment lent by a friend. She sat naked in bed with her lover, eating watermelon. When they heard tanks passing on the road outside, her lover rose and switched on the television: *Swan Lake* was on the screen, replacing the usual programmes with an endless parade of white tutus fluttering the alarm across a wide stage.

*

For the future's children and their fortune
For the highest mortal tribe
I lost my place at the fathers' feast
My gaiety, my pride.

How the years leap snarling onto my back
Though no wolf blood runs in my veins
Thrust me deep, as you'd thrust a hat
In the sleeve of Siberian plains.

*

Walter Benjamin watched *The Government Inspector* himself on 19 December 1926. It lasted over four hours, finishing at midnight, and Benjamin notes that it was 'non-dramatic', an observation that fills me with sympathy. I picture him arriving just before eight, taking off his coat and galoshes in the cloakroom, squeezing his hat into his coat sleeve before handing it all over to an attendant, and receiving a heavy wooden tag in return. It was not a cold December, but the pavements were still a choppy sea of ice and his shoes were damp. He checks his appearance in the long mirrors: a slightly untidy man in shining round spectacles. At midnight, when the show finally comes down, he is buffeted by the throngs collecting their furs, greatcoats, felt coats, padded jackets, and he leaves the cloakroom last. I see him being scolded for dropping a galosh; or standing in front of the mirror to drag his arm through his coat sleeve, forgetting his hat was lodged there.

*

Benjamin knew *The Government Inspector* and went alone to the theatre that night. Usually Asja, the woman he loved, or Bernhard Reich, her lover and companion, translated for him in the theatre. It's tiring work. I know, because I've done a lot of sitting by non-Russian speakers in theatres, explaining the narrative in a hissing whisper, to the fury of everyone around us.

*

Asja Lācis, a Communist and theatre practitioner, his collaborator, the woman he loved and to whom he had dedicated *Einbahnstrasse* (*One-Way Street*):

> DIESE STRASSE HEISST
> ASJA-LACIS-STRASSE
> NACH DER DIE SIE
> ALS INGENIEUR
> IM AUTOR DURCHGEBROCHEN HAT

In the poetic lines of his dedication the writer's creative brain is a city with a street named after Asja, the loved one. She is also the engineer who breaches (durchbricht) the space to drive a new street through. *Einbahnstrasse* was published in 1928, but Benjamin brought the work to Moscow to show Asja, giving her a copy of the handsome photomontage cover by Sasha Stone.

*

Benjamin comes onto the city's stage, under the glare of carbide, a backdrop of churches where pogroms might have been hatched, to play in a nightmarish three-hander: Asja, Bernhard Reich, Benjamin. All four walls are intact in this staging. There is no escape. The air is filled with smoke.

> Benjamin short-circuits his reading lamp.
> Benjamin waits for Asja in the cold.
> Benjamin eats far too much cake.
> Benjamin won't buy her an expensive fur,
>   but he buys himself all manner of lacquered toys.
> Benjamin rushes out of the room.
> Child Benjamin can never get off the tram at the
>   right stop because of the tight
>   press of furry bodies in the tramcar.
> Benjamin comes home triumphantly with a candle.

*

Gogol was given the subject of his 1835 play by Pushkin. In a letter to Pushkin, Gogol promises to make the play 'funnier than the devil'.

A small and remote provincial town is waiting for the arrival of a government inspector from the capital, St Petersburg. The town is corrupt, its officials are incompetent, criminal, desperately worried they will be exposed. When Khlestakov, a hungry young flibbertigibbet, arrives in the town and is taken for the inspector, he is quick to exploit the situation.

Khlestakov has a wonderful monologue on city life which unfolds from his mouth like a surreal contraption, clause after clause, like a confection, a vast layer cake. He's a liar who knows what his audience wants to hear, a skinny proto-Trump, who constructs rickety delight like a scaffold from which bodies will subsequently dangle:

'On the table, let's say, a melon, a melon costing seven hundred roubles. Soup in a tureen straight from Paris on a ship. You lift the lid and the steam – well there's nothing like it in all nature. I'm at balls day and night. We even have our own whist party at balls, the Minister of Foreign Affairs, the French Ambassador, the English one, the German one and me. I can quite wear myself out playing whist, it's like nothing else...'

*

The epigraph of Gogol's *The Government Inspector*:
На зеркало неча пенять, коли рожа крива
No point blaming the mirror if your face is crooked.

*

I set out to walk to the metro station Yugo-Zapadnaya, at the end of the red line. Thirty-five years ago it was still on the outskirts of the city. I walked a lot in Moscow on wintery days in the early nineties, miles and miles every day. The walk took me south down the broad pavements of Leninsky Prospect. The Moscow I knew was the Stalinist and postwar Moscow: monstrous blocks occupying whole streets; apartments with high stucco ceilings, built before the decree on ceiling height; wide avenues broken by engineers and surveyors through the neural maze of alleys and low wooden buildings.

The snow is heaped up along the sides of the avenue and coated in a sooty dust, the road itself is iron-grey asphalt. There are very few foreign cars and the traffic still looks like a Soviet postcard: trolleybuses with their grasshopper-leg trolley poles; snub-nosed jangling buses and Kamaz trucks. I pass a bread shop with a very long queue waiting outside on the pavement. A shop woman opens the door very slightly in order to unlock it, and then lets it crash shut again in the faces of the shoppers.

*

I do not think Benjamin walked around Moscow for pleasure. He walked the streets like a creature with compound eyes, noting and recording. I think he walked around Moscow with the clearsightedness of the abject, the erotically disturbed, the displaced, the angelic.

Benjamin notes that the shop signs indicate what is for sale with a simple word or a picture. No brands or glossy advertising. In 1991 the same is still true: bread, cheese, watch menders, umbrella repair, meat.

He is drawn to Moscow's cakes. Fantastic foamy creations, frosted with spun sugar and bright icing, laid out in drab shop windows. He even compares a scene in Meyerhold's production to the architecture of a cake. Such a Moscow comparison! The cakes in the nineties had names to match their grandeur: Napolean, Prague, Bird's Milk, Natasha, Kiev. The roses and ribbons of fondant icing were so sticky sweet that it seemed to me they weren't really for eating, they were for giving and receiving and decorating the table. Shop assistants deftly popped them into oblong boxes and parcel-wrapped them in brown paper and string, looping the string into a handle to carry away.

*

I was walking because I walked almost every day, filled with an anxiety I could only alleviate in perpetual movement. Once out of the apartment there was nowhere to perch so I would trudge along, thinking my million thoughts which, like starlings, would come together into whirling clumps and then disperse, unrecorded.

I can't remember the thoughts. Only the smells.

> tobacco
> urine
> aftershave
>
> mould
> mazut
> grease
>
> the feel of shallow slippery steps into
>   underpasses on the soles of my feet
> the sight of grimy bags on shopping trolleys
> the cold

*

When I walked I thought of Moscow as a snowglobe, the city rising out of the earth's curvature in a layering of lace and skirts. Place a telescope against the curved glass of the globe and you can see, very far away, a kiosk of chrysanthemums lit from inside like a stage.

*

Just beyond Yugo-Zapadnaya I came across a privately-owned restaurant and I was tired and cold so I went in. The restaurant was called *Habana*, a nod to the Socialist Brotherland that supplied the sugar for Moscow's cakes. The name was exotic, it promised warmth. I could cautiously enter such a curious and expensive place on my own – never with anyone I knew.

Benjamin found Moscow expensive, he didn't have enough money, but I recognised in his notes on Moscow the bewilderment at the value of money: he buys little treats and items, visits cafés and canteens, brings his toys and boxes back to the sanatorium where Asja is a patient – and suddenly has not enough cash to get home to Germany.

Currency from the outside world was stuffed deep in my inside pocket like a little bomb. The small amount of money I had saved as a teenager was a wealth in this momentarily sealed economy and I could in theory buy anything I wanted in Soviet shops: wooden skis, coffee sets, solid gold earrings. In fact my actual purchases were childlike, as were Benjamin's: postcards, wooden souvenirs, Christmas tree toys.

We both witnessed a tiny slice of history, a mere millisecond when a sealed globe was breached and the air outside and the fluid inside began to merge and mix and pollute each other. With the strange impediment of two heads, one pointing outwards, the other in, I could see the past and the future colliding like tectonic plates. I watched the wreckage piling up.

*

I went into *Habana* and ordered a coffee. It was beyond the means of my friends and I couldn't rid myself of the feeling I was doing something underhand. I must have divested myself of my heavy, childish garb in the cloakroom, my bright head scarf, which had a lambswool crocheted shawl doubled inside for warmth; my shapeless sheepskin.

I sat reading. There were tiny triangles of paper napkin on the table. Other than this I remember very little. Perhaps I walked home, perhaps I took the metro – the day folds into a thousand others.

*

When I recently went online to check whether this restaurant had actually existed, I found only an account describing it as the watering hole of the district's gangsters and racketeers in the early nineties. The article described how gangsters would leave their guns with their coats in the restaurant cloakroom, safe in the knowledge that the local police would tip off the management if they or another gang were planning a raid.

These small-town gangsters were tubby men with moustaches, knitted sweaters and leather coats. They looked like the flabby-faced functionaries of *The Government Inspector*. They belong with the spider-plants, fatty soups and marbled-floored foyers of the period.

*

Commerce flourished in the mid-twenties as a result of the New Economic Policy: kiosks sprang up in the streets, makeshift bazaars lit brightly by carbide lamps, selling all manner of produce, Christmas baubles, flowers, handmade ornaments. Mongolians stood in a line selling briefcases; speculators; women with pockets of meat.

Benjamin often drags his companions into shops, or is dragged past them himself with a child's grasping eyes, glancing back, trying to remember where the shop is so he can return alone to examine these dreams of colour and minute form. He is palpably excited by what is being traded: 'cloth and fabric form buttresses and columns', its surreal variety.

In the early 1990s the aisles of sellers and stalls around the metro had the architectonic function of spokes – sodden gangways leading you to the station at the hub of the wheel. Men and women in bulky coats stood in lines with laundry bags between their legs: stockings and tracksuits; make-up; alcohol; cake; fried meat pies, each folded in a scrap of paper; an old man standing in the sleety rain, holding out a single packet of cigarettes. Then commerce spilled itself into all places, it evolved, splitting cells, reproducing and forming new organisms, inhabiting basement offices, institutional foyers, bare earth patches of park, ledges, anywhere a seller could find purchase and purchaser. And with it came the racketeers, the gangs that controlled the markets, the Jesus pamphleteers, the Black Hundreds, the fakeries, the speculators, the grim smell of survival.

*

Yet Benjamin writes: 'It is precisely this transformation of an entire power structure that makes life here so extraordinarily meaningful. It is as insular and as eventful, as impoverished and yet in the same breath as full of possibilities as gold rush life in the Klondike.'

*

Irrepressible vitality. I come to write it up and it reproaches me. I am looking at this life from outside and containing it, but nothing in my life in Russia has ever been containable. It opens in front of me, wry, mocking, more than me. It writes *me* up.

*

In the days after the putsch I went with my friends to pro-democracy demonstrations. To see the new Federal flag over the Kremlin in place of the red flag of the USSR. We ended up at Lyubyanka, the building of the Secret Police, to see the toppled statue of the murderous 1920s secret police chief Felix Dzerzhinsky. A crowd of elderly protesters with placards and plastic bags stood outside the building, but I paid them scant attention and to this day I don't know what they actually felt about Dzerzhinsky's toppling.

*

Benjamin travels to Moscow with an unresolved dilemma. He is wondering whether to join the Party. Joining the Party would give him more work, he notes. But he wonders about a central paradox in Russian Communism which amounts to this: the postwar restoration of bourgeois cultural values meant they were being popularised in 'precisely the bleak, distorted guise for which, in the end, imperialism is to be thanked.'

*

One day I went into the main bedroom of the apartment to close a banging window. The walls were lined with years of Soviet literary periodicals and there was an old ornate mirror on a dressing table. All that writing. I sat on the corner of the bed in a room of print and stared into the mirror and suddenly it all struck me: I had arrived in the Soviet Union and it had suddenly disappeared.

A teenager sat in someone else's bedroom, and looked at the debris around her, the literary periodicals mounting skyward.

Every day I saw it in a different light and I thought there would be a resting point, a point at which I would conquer space and conceive it, and from that point I would emerge. I didn't know I was witnessing a disappearance and that, when I began to write, it would all be gone.

*

When we recall our earlier lives, when we fish moments from our own history, are we able to see these moments through the eyes we had then, or are the memories transfigured as they rush to the surface of our consciousness? Does this rushing transfiguration corrupt and destroy the intact memory? We see what we saw then – but we see it through our now-eyes, and with our now-thoughts, and so actually we no longer see what we once saw, and never will again.

Recalling past experience is like exposing an undeveloped film to light.

*

Meyerhold's 1926 production of *The Government Inspector* was, according to Benjamin, in line with a policy of using classic texts to overcome a 'catastrophic lack of education' in the Soviet population. Its failure was a politically important one.

Not all the criticism is political: Viktor Shklovsky comments acidly that the feedback form should have asked 'which act did you leave in?'. He writes that he held on till the bitter end, like an Eskimo waiting for a seal to pop out of a hole in the ice: alas no seal appeared.

But a number of prominent cultural figures defended the production. The writer Andrei Bely saw it as a tragedy, an interpretation that could not have been made in the Russia of Tsars Nikolai I or II. Meyerhold had brought Gogol into the twentieth century. 'It is not the real Government Inspector who arrives at the end,' writes Bely, 'but the future.'

*

If the real Government Inspector is the future, then the past is petrified under his stern gaze. Gogol's original play ends with an extended 'mute' scene – after the announcement of the real Inspector's arrival, the final stage direction states that the cast hold their positions 'petrified' for nearly a minute and a half.

However in Meyerhold's final *coup de théâtre* the cast leave the stage to music, dancing out of the auditorium. The coming of the real Inspector is announced as the curtain lifts again on a stage of unmoving wooden puppets.

*

That was me! I see it now. I stared and stared and could not speak. The future arrived in 1991 and I watched it, but failed to write it. It gradually became the past, and still I failed to write it. And now, by and large, it is barely spoken of, this vital, shame-filled interval between the snarling years.

But those of us who saw it and felt it, carry it within ourselves. I spent much of it walking the streets, always walking, seeing it with the same compound eye as Benjamin, but an eye unmoored, a language building itself. If I can say very little about it, then it is because I am partly made by it, this abject-erotic confection of dirty snow and fondant cream and tobacco and the suddenness of an evening blizzard.

Notes:
Benjamin, Walter, *Moscow Diary*, translated by Richard Sieburth and edited by Gary Smith (Harvard University Press, 1986)

Glück, Louise, *Proofs and Theories* (Carcanet, 1999)
Мейерхольд в русской театральной критике: 1920–1938 (Meyerhold in Russian theatre criticism: 1920–1938), edited by T. V. Lanina (Артист. Режиссер. Театр, 2000)

Two opening stanzas from Osip Mandelstam's poem 'За гремучую доблесть грядущих веков' in my translation. Gogol's *Ревизор* (*The Government Inspector*) is freely accessible online and quotes from the original are in my translation.

Poems

A.E. STALLINGS

Tree Buds

Buds are bombs
Which is to say
Their large inside
Is shut away,

Their small outside
A clenched fist,
The geode
To the amethyst.

As large as life
Their huge green hands
Lie folded up
In orisons,

Lie in the lap
Of luxury,
With sap and spring
Resurgent. See –

Each species pleated
In unique
Origami
Tight, sleek,

Like napkins at
Formal repasts,
The palisades
Of chloroplasts

Like scaled wings
In the chrysalis,
Palmate, lobed,
It comes to this,

Shaped like a blade,
Or cuneiform,
The pages leafed through
In a storm,

All coiled in this
Enamelled box:
The viridescent
Equinox,

Great summer's tent,
Turned gold and brown
When autumn's circus
Shakes it down,

And winter, with
His runic script,
To which all luscious
Cursive's stripped.

The universe
Was such a bud
Unfurling stars
And bones and blood,

And love and time
And every branch
Of evolution's
Avalanche,

The orchard's cool,
The serpent's dapple
Camouflage,
Dependent apple,

The gold sword
Of the cherubim,
Synecdoche
And metonym,

All held once
In a genie's lamp,
Where newness slept,
Raw, tender, damp.

Buds are bombs
Though they contain
Nothing louder
Than shade's refrain,

Nothing brighter
Than first blush,
Desirous and
Deciduous –

From little nodes
Whole worlds explode,
The paeon in
The palinode.

Buds are bombs,
Though when they burst,
No one is hurt.
(Or not at first.)

The Shadow Conductor

for Tom Smail

We sat braced for new music. On the stage,
Percussionists, strings, clarinet. The young
Conductor with her braid
Wound tightly, took her military post.
We only saw her back, her shoulders square
As epaulets; from arms akimbo swung

The gnomon of her brisk baton. Through air
She sliced, and in between the silences,
Black notes in murmuration
Flocked and changed direction, startled, stopped.
She kept a time too intricate to count,
Her discipline, yes that was paramount,

Her spine impassive, and her motions, cropped.
But then we saw that in the corner moved
A wraith scrawled on the wall
In cancelled light, lithe torso, arms like boughs,
A silhouetted face that seemed to shout
Or sing, a wand that fell before the fall

Of every beat – conductor of the shades
To deeper, darker halls. That's when we saw
Not quick obedience,
But music as foreshadowing, a flaw
Of lighting showed us, past the barricades
Of logic, lie such passions glimpsed askance

As these gesticulations, furious
Directions, and the shapes cast by the sound.
The mallets and the bows,
How instruments of adumbration dance
To cadences we've scarcely understood.
Our hands flap as fresh quiets discompose.

From the Book of Disorderly Days

A Letter from Japan

GREGORY O'BRIEN

Ichihara

It takes me back to the slippery, water-resistant English town of Buxton, January 2024, and the glassy pond upon which pedal-boats and swans went about their separate yet oddly syncopated manoeuvres. One particularly decrepit, half-sinking pedal-boat on Buxton Pond bore a wishful, handwritten imperative: 'Half Price Half Hourly Rental', an offer for which, sensibly, there were no takers. My wife Jen and I are presently on the foreshore of the well-manicured Ichihara Lake, east of Tokyo City. A poem by Tokyo-based New Zealander Brent Kininmont – whom we met a few days ago – sets this scene for us, or revisits it: 'Across the pond the wind has swept / the swan boats into a jam…'

With their polished white hulls and rounded rooftops, from which protrude swannish necks and long-beaked heads, the two-person pedal-boats of Ichihara appear lake-worthy and well-appointed for both maritime and faux-avian roles. (The actual swans of the prefecture appear to have been relegated to adjacent waterways and lesser tributaries.) The flotilla of swan-boats Brent encounters in his recently published collection, *The Companion to Volcanology*, is far less mobile than those laid out before us. In one poem, the usually bustling pondlife is frozen in a Tokyo-style gridlock:

> Neck and neck, couples
> and small families going nowhere.
> Swimming out is not an option –
> the signs are clear on this.
> One soaked woman cradling a child
> has reached her limit. *See!*
> It's only up to her knees.

Brent lives mostly in Tokyo but also rents a small apartment in the west of Honshu, on the coast not far from Hiroshima – a place at once swimmable and writable – where he houses his collection of books. We imagine Brent speeding westwards on the Shinkansen for an immersion in both the Sea of Japan and the sea of literature. On a Lucky Tuesday in April, he might even find himself riding the 'Adorable Train', the pink-striped Hello Kitty Shinkansen which wends its way through the well-appointed cherry orchards between Osaka and Hiroshima.

Similarly adorable, the J-pop group Muse is scheduled to appear later today at Tower Records, back in Shibuya. Hence the boisterous gathering of signature hunters jamming the pavement outside. The nine-member band is a recasting of the Nine Muses of Ancient Greece, although their concept and output – recent releases include 'Love Wing Bell' backed with 'Dancing Stars on Me!' – would likely prove resistant to further exegesis.

The nine muses of Ancient Greece (in no particular order): Calliope (epic poetry), Clio (history), Euterpe (music), Thalia (comedy), Melpomene (tragedy), Erato (lyrical poetry), Polyhymnia (hymns), Urania (astronomy), and Terpsichore (dance).

It was the band's fanbase, by way of a cellphone poll, that decided the group's name. Originally all nine 'muses' had been employed as voice actors in an anime series. From their voice-roles, they sprang into real life – a rare case of actual people emerging out of cartoon characters: life imitating art, although – in its way – at the same time remaining 'art'. Or disembodied voices becoming – on a speculative, managerial whim – profitably embodied.

Maybe the literary historian Rosa Campbell's remark that 'the muse is not a speaking role' needs a caveat, allowing for a possible singing role for said muse(s) within the noisy genre of J-Pop: high-pitched and expressionless, and propelled onwards by an incessant backing track: a bouncy, musical Shinkansen. In contradiction to all prevailing myths involving muses and male poets, not a single boy or man is to be found among the fans hammering on the glass frontage of Tower Records.

Kyoto

'Even in the concrete, *things are happening*.' My artist friend Robin White is studying the paving between her slippered feet and the hyper-organised formation of insects as they go about their insect business. (Prefiguring Robin's remark, her recent retrospective exhibition at the Museum of New Zealand was titled 'Something is happening here'.) We are visiting the house of her kindred spirit, the artist-potter-philosopher Mr Kanjiro Kawai of Kyoto. Located at the rear of his house (which is now a museum) is an enormous Angama or 'Climbing Dragon' kiln, of a kind which originated in China around the fifth century. An ungainly beast, it is also majestic in an arcane, medieval way. A sputtering, glowing, proudly pre-industrial habitation for fire and clay, it also reminds me of the church organ celebrated in Henry Purcell's 'Ode to Saint Cecilia' – a 'wondrous machine' well-purposed for the consolidation of the community and for building social cohesion.

I find myself immediately drawn to the potter – not only to the industry of the man but also the fact he went through a lengthy period of crippling self-doubt and depression, during which he gave up pottery and turned to writing poetry and essays in which he imparted a typically distilled Oriental wisdom...

'Nothing is –
Look, and it is.'

... as plainly stated and grounded as the Mingai pottery movement with which he is associated:

I am you,
The you that only I can see.

Eventually he found his way back to ceramics again, reacquainting himself with the Anagama kiln, in the warm company of which he lived out his very productive days. On this April afternoon, his house museum is open to visitors who step lightly through his dwelling, pilgrim-like and respectful, taking care not to topple anything or wake the sleeping cat on the tatami matting. Alongside the rustic forms of the philosopher-potter's ceramic musings, there are numerous calligraphies hanging from the walls or displayed in cabinets.

I have been re-reading *The Pillow Book of Sei Shonagon*, Arthur Waley's version, in which 'the cult of calligraphy' is discussed. In tenth-century Japan, 'beauty of penmanship' was considered nearly as important as 'beauty of person'. It was often deemed a virtue rather than a talent, the *Pillow Book* notes, 'and the epithet "good", when applied to an individual, frequently referred not to conduct but to handwriting... Often in Japanese romances it is with some chance view of the heroine's writing that a love-affair begins.'

Pillow Book
A non-existent breeze enters through
   the open window of
      a non-existent shrine. The non-existent bride
        sweeps
the last filaments
   from the sun-lit corner of
a non-existent
     marriage. The non-existent emperor of a
non-existent country
   writes a song in praise of
his 7000 non-existent concubines, all of them
present and unaccounted for –
   just like this evening's
non-existent clouds
   if slightly less
     furtive,
        irrepressible... Non-existent steps of
a non-existent dance
   with a non-existent noblewoman. And much
   later
the non-existent body laid out
   in its non-existent coffin.

But why then this weight upon us –
   that consumes
     but will not
deliver us? And why then
is everyone here gathered
   so visibly shaken, inconsolable?

Teshima
'Every time I view the sea, I feel a calming sense of security as if visiting my ancestral home', writes the photographer/artist Hiroshi Sugimoto. 'I embark upon a voyage of seeing.' This afternoon, the Inland Sea – so beloved of Sugimoto and so often pictorialized in his large-format photographs – is mirror-calm and pondlike, interrupted only by the occasional freighter. At a remote extremity of the sparsely populated island of Teshima, the French artist Christian Boltanski has created his own 'pilgrimage site' – a beachfront pavilion containing a single artwork/concept. Visitors to *Les Archives du Coeur* are invited, for a modest fee, to have their heartbeat recorded and then filed away in the artist's 'library', where future visitors can search for it by name or city of origin.

In the darkness of the corridor-like 'Heart Room' inside the pavilion, a single lightbulb hangs in pitch-blackness, flickering in time with a succession of recorded heartbeats, extracted at random from an archive which now contains some 600,000 sound-files. What strikes us most is the immense variety: one heartbeat is a bass drum, another a floor being swept... the ticking of an underwater clock... a door being blown open and shut... a murmur... Later I don a set of headphones in the 'Listening Room' and sample the on-line files, discovering along the way that six people named Christian Boltanski, from six different places, have left recordings of their heartbeats here – presumably only one of them the real Boltanski. Or none of them. Their heartbeats seem to have nothing in common with each other.

From a sound system outside the burnt-black wooden pavilion, a faint heartbeat is broadcast out across the surrounding environs. At the far end of the adjacent beachfront, an uncommonly tall Japanese man in a jet-black suit is performing a slow sequence of T'ai C'hi manoeuvres. We wonder if he is trying to synchronize his heartbeat with the one that is audible along the foreshore. And why is the broad-winged kite hovering so long over the beach – maybe to dive upon the warm-blooded source of the heartbeat when it finally wanders forth across open ground? Still within earshot of the pervasive sound, a woman is walking the foreshore, pausing every few minutes to uplift variously shaped pieces of seaweed – wakame – which she voraciously eats, smiling the whole time. On a bench, leaning against the outside wall of the structure, I am thinking about Janet Frame's short story 'You are now entering the human heart' and wondering about the literary implications/ possibilities of this place.

Mr Boltanski
A dark room
and we are inside
Mr Boltanski's
heart – its hillside pinked
with azaleas. Our own hearts
beat quietly inside
the caves
of our bodies,
while Mr Boltanski's
fills our ears with a noise
like fear.

Thomas Abbot's heart
we cannot hear
at all.
                    (Jenny Bornholdt)

The smallest room in *Les Archives du Coeur*, the 'Listening Room' contains a slit-shaped window, across which the Inland Sea horizon extends – not unlike the flat-line on a heart monitor beside a hospital bed. It is that detail which sets me thinking about Pope Francis, whose heartbeat, at this moment in time, is becoming fainter in a hospital bed in Vatican City.

And then I wonder if there might be further variations and avenues to be explored by Boltanski's archive, which also presents itself as a laboratory in which all the staff wear white lab coats and wield clipboards. Maybe one day the archive will include a database of what people are thinking when their heartbeats are being recorded? Or who, among the living and the dead, they are remembering? Or who they are in love with? Maybe the subjects could be recorded while reciting a poem. There might be other rhythms to preserve. Iambics of the poetic heart. Perhaps the public could be given an opportunity, upon listening to the sound of a particular heart, to reassign it to a fictional or historical character. Or to a person who doesn't exist yet. Imposter heartbeats... It becomes more and more like a Janet Frame story.

Walking back along the beach, another question remains unanswered: whose heartbeat was it playing on the speaker system outside the building? Boltanski's?

Naoshima
Jen and I have been staying with others at the Ippukudyaya, a guest house amidst a bamboo forest on Naoshima Island. Early on the first morning, a raccoon dog or tanuki came scuttling out of the bamboo grove and stepped gingerly towards where I was sitting, sketchbook in hand, overlooking a small lake. Despite its status in Japanese folklore as a trickster and shape-shifter, the creature is surprisingly sociable and trusting, which is especially surprising given the uncomfortable fact that tanuki hair is sought after for its use in calligraphy brushes. The tanuki returned on the second day with four others. A conclave. On this occasion he came right up and nipped my foot – a signal, presumably, that he was expecting to be fed.

On this, the third morning, when we are about to catch the ferry back to Honshu, five tanuki appear beside the driveway, evenly spaced and forming an impromptu guard of honour as we drive back to the main road. Meanwhile, in Rome the Pope is also, by latest accounts, about to set forth on a trajectory onwards and outwards, with Papal Guards instead of raccoon dogs in attendance. Each of us, in turn, departing our island for another, further island.

Like his namesake St Francis of Assisi, the Pope proposed, on numerous occasions, a spirituality bedrocked in 'a concern for nature, justice for the poor, commitment to society, and interior peace'. In his 'apostolic exhortation', *Laudato si* (2015), he made the further point: 'Nothing in this world is indifferent to us'. Such an environmentally driven, holistic approach to human and non-human life is not unlike that of the founder of the art islands, Soichiro Fukutake, who continues to champion the cultural and social regeneration of rural areas – a philosophy laid out in his book *With Art As My Weapon*. 'A different and viable world exists in the boundless countryside', he writes. 'Our ancestors are there...' (I find his further conclusion that 'art has a greater impact when in the presence of agriculture' not only beguiling but delightful.) Mr Fukutake's thinking echoes not only Confucius but also Ezra Pound in one of his less woolly moments: 'Learn of the green world what can be thy place / in scaled invention or true artistry...'.

The news arrives, by way of someone's cellphone, that Pope Francis has died. We find ourselves staring upwards into the translucent sky, awaiting a cloud, a puff of smoke. A sign. A change in the weather. This morning would have been the perfect time to register Pope Francis's heartbeat in the Teshima Island archive: his final heartbeats, winding down, and then the silence after the final one.

Tsuta
The gods are in a continual state of being updated and renewed – so has it the handbook of the Benesse Art Site on Naoshima Island. 'Shinto shrines are generally remodelled continuously over generations to offer better dwelling to gods according to the aesthetics and technology of the time.'

Driving inland from Hiroshima one evening, my eye is caught by a number of giant carp which appear to be suspended mid-air beneath the ceiling of a roadside barn. They could be balloons or possibly floats for a springtime carnival or parade. In the Japanese scheme of things, the carp is considered a spirit-being and has long been associated with strength, perseverance and good luck. The most notable piece of good luck that befell the species itself was its awful taste; had it been delectable to the human palate, its revered status would not have been so easily granted. In the hillside villages, the fish exists in various forms: on the ridges of ceramic rooftops (*shachihoko*) and in folklore, where a *shachi* is a carp with the head of a lion or tiger or dragon. During previous centuries, samurai would keep ornamental carp – silver, gold, yellow – as a status object. The carp has never fared so well in Aotearoa New Zealand, where, in the Waikato region, there are annual competitions to see who can dispatch the greatest number of these overbearing invaders – a species held largely responsible for the laying waste of the native fish population. This yearly contest involves bows and arrows, as well as guns. At the end of the day, the mountainous harvest is consigned to a wood chipper and re-rendered as a fishy but effective fertiliser for the adjacent farmlands.

A little further along the road, I notice a snail – the Japanese symbol of tenacity and patience – the height of a two-storied dwelling. Both snail and carp I add to the index of gods encountered in recent days, alongside the high-heeled, disco-dancing minor deities outside Tower Records, Shibuya.

Hiroshima Mushroom Stall

All the things
you are –
umbrella, walking stick
folded kimono, lantern
bell, pair of earrings
slippers, hearing aid
snow drift, girl band –
all the things
a mushroom can be
when it is not
a cloud.

Off to one side of the village where we are staying – Tsuta, in the Hiroshima prefecture – there is a furniture factory – well-sited in this heavily wooded region. Just outside our house stands a modest roadside Buddha, decked out in a bright red woollen hat and vest. (I am told that it is to this well-tended statue that the villagers commend the safety and wellbeing of their children.) Visible from the room where I am sleeping is a small cave which, in past centuries, was used for storing crops over the winter months. In more recent times it has functioned as a bomb shelter, from which the residents emerged, cautiously, after the Hibaku – the atomic bombing of Hiroshima – before they headed into the city to look for relatives who had not come home.

Hiroshima

A perfect morning, flying above the Inland Sea – from my window seat, I watch as the coastal city of Hiroshima draws near and the inevitable thought comes to mind: 'This is exactly what it must have looked like for the pilot and crew of the B29 Enola Gay'. Eighty years after the A-Bomb, the sky above Hiroshima still feels sacrosanct. What few birds there are glide furtively over the War Memorial Park, hugging the treeline. A plaque has been installed on a nearby footpath to denote the epicentre of the explosion 600 metres directly above. These days, drones are banned from the sky above the city and, accordingly, from the reflection of that sky in the seventy-metre-long Peace Pond which is sited between the Hiroshima Peace Memorial (Genbaku Dome) and the Hiroshima Peace Memorial Museum. Signs all over the city remind visitors: NO DRONES IN HIROSHIMA. Neither are there aeroplanes to be seen directly above us.

Back in the hillside town, ankle-deep in cherry blossoms, we venture forth into the Disabled Forest, a carefully tended plantation through which wheelchair-accessible concrete paths have been constructed. White and pink blossoms infuse the air with a flickering, staccato energy – another kind of sky writing. Nature doing what it does. I am reminded of Fenollosa's assertion that 'the verb must be the primary fact of nature… the cherry tree is all that it does'. In an adjacent facility – the School of Benevolent Archery – access for the disabled is also a priority. In the Hiroshima prefecture, during the postwar period and still to this day, neither good health nor a full complement of limbs are ever presumed.

Hatsukaichi

A number of the works that the artist Robin White has made for the Hatsukaichi Cultural Centre were created collaboratively with the Hiroshima-based calligrapher Taeko Ogawa. Taeko devoted much of her earlier working life to teaching reading and writing to the survivors of the Hiroshima and Nagasaki bombings – the hiba - kusha – many of whom missed out on a formal education for health-related reasons. Reflecting on that experience, Taeko began some years ago to make large-scale calligraphic works, some of which are included in the current exhibition. Her works bear titles, or inscriptions, such as: 'Water, water, please give me water, I am a burning fire ball'. And, a little further along the gallery wall: 'This is the river where people died wanting water. Now we float candle lanterns to calm their spirits.'

The exhibition is part of an ongoing programme of events to commemorate the eightieth anniversary of Hibaku. Taeko comes into the gallery every day and talks with visitors, nearly all of whom have a personal connection with the atomic bomb. On the opening day, she offers a 'performance' in which she makes a large calligraphic work on scrolls of paper laid out on the gallery floor.

Taking her first step, her shoes removed, from the floorboards onto the unfurled paper, she is like someone wading into a pond of uncertain depth. Then, from nowhere, there is a bolt of energy and she is on the move: walking down each paper scroll, trailing calligraphic markings from her dripping tanuki brush. Her actions are accompanied by the plaintive sounds of a shakuhachi (Japanese wooden flute) which is being played by a musician less than two metres away. There is a sense that, in the Japanese schema, painting and writing exist *within* each other – and somehow music is also part of the internal workings of that process. The moment Taeko's brush first strikes the paper is like a bird diving into a pond, an explosive moment. From that point, it is a complete immersion – she is at the service of the paintbrush, its serious purpose. Some minutes later, the conclusion of the work is just as dramatic. When the brush finally withdraws abruptly from the paper, it is over. Over.

Coda

It is January 2024 and I am sitting between my friend Angel and my wife Jen in the Manchester jazz club, Band on a Wall. From the stage, the unexpectedly talkative jazz drummer Sebastian Rochfort starts explaining to the gathered crowd how playing the drums involves every other aspect of your life. And it follows that attending a concert should involve other parts of your life as well. Like everywhere you have been earlier in the day. Like who you are. Sebastian Rochfort has recently lost his father. How do you play that fact on a drum kit? How does a lifetime or a memory or even a moment enter and inhabit the process of art making? A patter, a crescendo, a flittering cymbal like a bird's wing brushing the surface of a lake? The crack of a snare-drum like a tanuki crashing through bamboo? (The accompanying pianist, Kit Downes, sitting silently at his instrument, is by now a part of the audience too.) As Sebastian continues, the mood in the room changes. Handles of Guinness are placed on the floor or bar. He asks all of us in the audience to close our eyes and focus on *the light-source that exists at the very core of our being.* In a solemn, respectful silence unlike any I have ever encountered before in a music venue, we are rendered motionless, imagining a light which radiates outwards from the depths of our bodies, from our hearts, beaming forth to illuminate those around us and the world beyond.

'And I come to the fields and spacious palaces of my memory, where are the treasures of innumerable images...'
(Saint Augustine)

Two Poems

SINÉAD MORRISSEY

Doggerland

To stop the waters　　　　　　　　　　　　　　　　rising
trailer sucker hopper dredgers　　　　　　hoover up the seabed
then jettison　　　　　　　　　　　　whatever they've trapped
sand　　　　　　　　　　　　　　　　　　　　　　　　　silt
aggregate　　　　　　　　　　　　　　　　　　　　rainbow it
in pummelling arcs　　　　　　　　　　　closer to the coast
widening the distance　　　　　　　　　　　a fingerbreadth
between sea　　　　　　　　　　　　　　　　and shoreline
between now　　　　　　　　　　　　　and what is coming
allsorts　　　　　　　　　　　　　spread out on the beaches
for an army of citizen　　　　　　　　　　　　　scientists
to brandish　　　　　　　　　　　　　　　　　as signposts
hammerstone flints　　　　　　　　　　　　　arrowheads
awls antler-axes　　　　　including their wooden handles
the entire toolkit　　　　　　　　　　　of the Mesolithic
perfectly preserved　　　　the skull of a young Neanderthal
you could walk from Leiden to London　　Berlin to York
not a bridge not a road not an outpost　its own flourishing
heart mammoth-steppe birch tarpitch rhinos　by the Rhine
thirteen thousand year-old decorated　　bison metatarsal
we're moving away from cave paintings　　　　　to art
that is almost abstract says the man　　　in the museum
zig-zagging lines like a migraine　　seismic reflection data
of petroleum geo-services　　　　　　　　　providing a map
The Spines The Outer　　　　　　　　　　　　Silver Pit
you could see Dogger Bank　　　　　　　　　　for miles
isostatic adjustment　　　　　　　　　　as the land began
to tilt　　　tundra marshland　　saltmarsh　　　islands
fast says the man　　　　　　　　　　　　*we're talking*
metres　　　　　　　　　　　　　　　　　*per generation*
tree stumps at Redcar　　　　　　　　　　　　footprints
visible for an instant　　　　　before the waves roll back

Painting *vs* Photograph

So where do you stand right now? On a globe
spinning at a thousand miles per hour around a sun
rotating at sixty thousand miles per hour inside
a solar system flying sideways at half a million
miles per hour within a galaxy whirling round
at a million miles per hour and you feel nothing?

I'm only asking a question. A lie is still a lie,
even if everyone believes it. An apple falling
on your head doesn't prove gravity. Look out to sea.
There should be hundreds of feet of curvature
between you and the horizon and there just isn't.
Jupiter doesn't even look like a planet.

The sun and moon are simply lights in the sky.
In reality, you are living in a giant planetarium
forward slash terrarium forward slash soundstage
forward slash Hollywood backlot that is so big
you, and everyone you know, and everyone
you've ever known, have never figured it out.

The Earth is more like Pangea than you think,
except ringed in a wall of ice. There are no known
flight paths in the Southern Hemisphere: the ocean's
too wide to cross. GPS doesn't work in Antarctica.
once you've seen the clues, it's a revelation –
how they've been lying to us all this time. NASA

means *to deceive* in Hebrew. Unlike other communities,
we're fundamentally positive. We make stuff.
Flat Earth clock. Flat Earth watch. Flat Earth glass-topped
coffee table. How could you sing a folk song
about 9/11? And if our families no longer speak to us,
it's not our fault. It's too big a paradigm shift.

He-that-shall-not-be-named says we're growing
*an anti-intellectual movement that will mean the end
of civilisation and democracy as we know it.*
For pointing out a simple flaw in the argument?
It's insane. But we *are* growing. We actually broke a million
videos last week. I mean physically. A million videos.

The sky's the limit.

In Dialogue with *Paris Spleen* by Baudelaire –

CSILLA TOLDY

Introduction
I was a refugee in Paris in 1981 and lived in the city for six months, and now, after forty-three years, while I was waiting for a test result that would tell me whether I had breast cancer, I returned as a writer in residence. I imagined a dialogue with the themes of *Paris Spleen* based on my memories as well as based on the present, but more from the female perspective.

The organising principle follows that of *Paris Spleen* by Baudelaire; fifty prose poems numbered. I start each poem of mine with an epigraph from Baudelaire's poem in Louise Varèse's translation (1890–1989; first published in 1947 with New Directions).

III
Artist's Confiteor
The study of beauty is a duel in which the artist shrieks with terror before being overcome.

The owners of my present home must be clowns. The many photos of street art on the walls make me smile. It was my dream job as a child.

While the musicians travelling with us on the metro get some money, sometimes the beggars are met with less compassion. An *accro* begged in sing-song French, pulling the strings of my heart – soft voice, like a baby. One foot in the shoe, the other half out. A young girl he approached said plainly 'no'. She had a clear, honest face and looked into his eyes meaning 'sort yourself out, I am poor, too'.

Die a little
Beauty hurts. It vibrates the lowest and highest strings of my being. I create, but I am never able to express it as perfectly as it is inside me. Each creation is just a step closer. One step closer to eternity.

When the artist shrieks with terror before being overcome, it is a *petit morte*.

Each of his creations is a little death.

XLI
Sea-ports
... people who still have enough energy to have desires, who still desire to voyage, who still desire to get rich.

At sea, again
But no, I am thinking of all the rejected refugees, who cannot stay in the city and then go to Calais in the hope of finding the narrowest passageway where they can get into boats and sail to England. Where did all that money for the traffickers come from? Why are you telling your child to board? What other way is there to live or die? Who will save you?

The constellations that guide you in the night or the rescue boats' horns as your aim – save us, please save us!

> flotsam-
> baby shoes
> no more

XLVI
Loss of a Halo
But aren't you going to advertise for your halo, at least? Or notify the police?

I walked down Île Saint Louis to find Hotel Lauzun, where Baudelaire lived. Certainly, there is a plate next to the entrance to call the fact to your attention, but when you step inside the building, a concierge stops you. She has no pity for your research, even though this is now an educational institution of some kind. Perhaps next time you will be allowed to see the inside, the Louis XIV gilded décor and statues? And you ask yourself: Will there be a next time? You leave and walk along the promenade, the river, where he liked to walk through the nights, talking to Jeanne Duval, feeling her soft arm in his, listening to the melody of the Seine and her voice humming its Haitian tune.

Ars Poetica
I don't have a halo. My granny had one. She made it for herself out of sacrifice.

> luminescent ring
> hovering above her
> toothless smile

My only praise is when my readers tell me that they could not put down the book or it 'sucked' them in. I am not complicated, or celebrated, I just do what I like and what I was meant to do.

It took a long time to get here, but my *ars poetica* is in the art of avoiding ridicule, even if I want to make people laugh. My earliest memories of society are bullying and being laughed at. I made it into an art at home, entertaining my grieving parents and sisters. *Le Bouffon* who makes comedy out of misery. On the other side, society presented autocrats. Autocrats do not have humour, only power – but they will always pass.

Laughter liberates and they are ridiculed, big time!

XLVII
Miss Bistouri
I am passionately fond of mystery because I always hope to discover the solution. So I let myself be piloted by this chance companion, or rather by this unhoped-for enigma.

Enigma
Today, I visited Musée Jacquemart André and amongst the wealth of art this couple collected and the wonderful interiors, design, the winter garden with its double spiral staircase, the exhibition of la Galerie Borghese – my poignant discovery was that Jacquemart died of syphilis. So many, including Baudelaire and my Hungarian poet idol, Ady, prominent and definitely less prominent members of nineteenth- and early twentieth-century societies died of this disease. It did not spare nobility, rich or poor – together with TB, it made sure that people died in their sixties at the latest. It seems certain that the little prostitutes who could not survive unless they sold their bodies, starting in their teens, as well as the general promiscuity of society made a sexually transmitted disease so virulent.

In *XLVII*, Baudelaire talks about a mad woman who mistakes him for a doctor and wants to be cured by him. Madness, perhaps a strain or symptom of syphilis?

> surreal fever
> acrobatic minds submerged
> in holy visions

The other day, on the bus, a man of about sixty – although I am not sure of old men's ages – sat before me. He talked, and I had to check a few times whether he had an earpiece or an earphone in his ears because an implement like that can cause people to babble into thin air, nowadays. But no, he was addressing an invisible person to his left with some animation. They argued about – who knows – it seemed to be some hurt, and of course, he was in the right. After a while, he started to gesticulate over his right shoulder towards me, as if I was the enemy, sitting behind him, and I was relieved when the man got off the bus near St. Ouen at last.

XLVIII
Anywhere out of the world
Life is a hospital where every patient is obsessed by the desire of changing beds.

When the soul desires darkness and you feel you could live anywhere. A desire to move – to be somewhere else – to live somewhere else – and the wise child, who is sensing the proximity of death, wants to 'go home'.

Where is this home? For me, it must be in the sky and in light, not the sun's or the moon's reflected but white, otherworldly, not the neon of films with aliens, but thinner and softer, shimmering. And then I can fly and perhaps be embraced by a motherly love in the dark as if back in the womb.

I am not sure I could endure another life.

Pilgrimage to the Mater
She tripped over a stone on her way. As if it had to appear again and remind her of the... of the one in her left breast. She was on her way.

Now that she started to talk to it, she discovered that it could be an elongation of her heart, a petrified extension of a shock or trauma that her heart could not carry or bear to take on. Now exported, exuded into the soft tissue, the mammary gland that used to feed her babies, now a stone that she wanted to throw away as far as she could.

Her iris with its many rays expanded too, in all directions, like the English sun over Edwardian doorways. *We took the language and perfected it*, she thought, *and I took the stone under my tongue, like Cicero.*

'May the sun shine warm upon your face' she kept repeating. Her voice turned inward, humming to her stone, while her environment thought she was a mad Irish woman on her way to the Mater, where babies are born.

    her tongue tied
    into another womb
    mute again

XLIX
Beat up the poor
A man is the equal of another only if he can prove it, and to be worthy of liberty a man must fight for it.

We are here for the art

As a twist of fate, my new neighbours are quarrelling, loud Hungarians – a mother and daughter, as I can figure from their noise. This house's walls are thin, and tiny studios are rented out through Airbnb. I was safe enough here, like they will be as tourists in this city, where all nationalities reside and try to survive.

My nails are done by Philippinos, dinner made by Chinese, Spanish or Italian people, my safety provided by French (I still have not seen a black policeman although there is a strong police presence in the streets), my bin emptied by French-Africans or French-Arabs. We are here in this beautiful melting pot of art and culture; I could just about survive on the £25.00 per diem that the Arts Council allows, and yet I feel that I have a rich life.

Beating up the poor happens elsewhere.

I watch rich, lonely widows walking the streets. Doting French mothers who have rendezvous with their sons in museums. The French crème de la crème who need to admire the *chefs-d'oeuvres* of Caravaggio, Leonardo, Raphael, Bellini, Rubens, Titian and do it all in silence, whispering and murmuring their acknowledgement, not to be disturbed. Respect the admiration, the enjoyment of art, they all paid to get into this wonderful exhibition.

Beating up the poor happens elsewhere.

    In chains
    the Burghers of Calais –
    don't go there.

In Galerie La Moulinette a pop-up exhibition where artists write poems for walkers-by. Poetry is made here and playfulness is our privilege. Matthieu Dufour mates words to add another layer, such as 'sireine' translated into 'sireign' – the mating of a mythical creature and a queen – or aubessolète, where the word 'sun' and 'obsolete' indicate that things of the night become obsolete when the sun's first rays touch them. All of this is given to me by D. with a smile. I promise to come back, *au-revoir*.

    made up language
    try to be modern –
    L'art pour l'art?

L
The Faithful Dog
'To M. Joseph Stevens who painted Folette'
And every time he puts down the painter's waistcoat he is forced to think of faithful dogs, and of Indian Summers and the beauty of women past their prime.

Folette
I desire a dog, too. At a certain age, we women 'past our prime' desire one to cherish and love – who would not push us away but needed our little gestures, caresses, scratches and, shamefully, a myriad of kisses.

Alone in the world – as one might say – but no, we have friends, other abandoned women who like a jack-in-a-box stood up and survived every blow. They call in the middle of the night and enquire about our wellbeing and say, we are an inspiration, caressing our little soul, just at the right time.

    in turbulent times
    walk on water
    holding hands

Do Birds Sing?

LESLEY HARRISON

I live in Angus on the east coast of Scotland, above the big fjords of the Forth and Tay, just where the land starts to lean out into the North Sea. Around 6200 BC, a massive failure of the Norwegian continental shelf caused a giant tsunami which swept south and west for hundreds of miles, reaching our coastline in a matter of hours, swamping estuaries and river valleys and barging far inland. As it seeped back, in what had been the soft, grassy bed of a slowing burn, it left a wide scooped-out bowl. The Montrose Basin is now a vast, almost entirely enclosed expanse of slab and mudflat. Twice a day when the tide comes in, it is a shallow, temporary sea.

Needless to say it bristles with birdlife: all migrant species of the North Atlantic are present, sometimes en masse. Each October around 100,000 pinkfoot geese make landfall here as they head south from Iceland and the Faroes. Their call, clear amid the rattling of thousands of wings, is a streaming 'ink-ink' – giving rise maybe to their local name: *kwink*. There is a very satisfying glimpse here of the moment that the bird was named; of someone trying to fit their mouth to what they heard in their landscape, tuning consonants and vowels until they arrived at a deft, self-explanatory sound-image of that thing over there, that creature whose arrival alters the soundscape so significantly, and leaves with such clamour.

Such words have currency. Bird lists for countries round the North Sea rim show a similar attention to sound – the first and easiest means of identifying them at distance – and to sound-in-place. *Kwink* is also used of the greylag and Brent goose, *klekk* or *claikis* of the barnacle goose (less of a chiming, more of a squawk). Old Norse, the language of the Vikings and ancestor of modern Scandinavian languages, is also the root of many peculiarly Shetlandic, Orcadian and Scots words. Names, like the birds, also crossed the North Sea. A seagull is a *maa* in Orkney and a *meeuw* in the Netherlands; the curlew a *whaup* in Caithness and Berwick and a *wulp* on the mudflats at Westhoek. And if you string their names together, you can almost hear the birds arriving and settling on these northern beaches as the tide turns and their feeding grounds are exposed:

fulmar	*mallimak – maali – mallemuk – qaqulluk*
kittiwake	*facky – kitto – rittock – rita – krykkje*
golden plover	*weeo – hjelje – heidloa – ló – heilo*
redshank	*pleep – weeweep – stellit – stelkur – tureluur*

The idea of a language of the birds was already old when it appeared in Norse myth. This was the belief that birdsong and human speech were sometimes so close that certain gifted individuals could cross from one to the other. This is a seductive theory. In 1857, hauling through the Pentland Firth aboard the *Fox*, Captain Francis McClintock likened the 'hoarse screams and unintelligible dialect' of the Orkney pilots to the sound of the sea birds that mobbed them, 'as if we had suddenly awoke in Greenland itself'. And in the online database *Tobar an Dualchais/Kist o Riches*, two recordings from the late 1950s demonstrate an old established belief in the adjacency of human and bird song. In wax cylinder recordings, Mrs Annie Johnston of Barra integrates the 'conversation' of the thrush, the lark, the crow, the gull and the dove into her own Gaelic. In another, her husband, Mr Calum Johnston, sings a Pilliù, an ancient *caoine* or keening song. The Pilliù mimics the long call and syllables of the redshank. Of these kinds of singing, says ethnologist Mairi McFadyen, 'the dividing lines between bird-song, music and speech are impossible to determine'.

Poets and writers have long been alert to the blurry synthesis of language and landscape. In *A Part of Speech*, Joseph Brodsky describes the Baltic marshland of his childhood with its 'zinc-grey breakers that marched on / in twos. Hence all rhymes, hence the wan flat voice'. Norman MacCaig's Aunt Julia spoke her Hebridean Gaelic with 'a seagull's voice', her speech and movement growing out of the very matter of her island-world:

> She was buckets
> and water flouncing into them.
> She was winds pouring wetly
> round house-ends.

Shetland poet Roseanne Watt talks of 'writing in two languages', English and Shaetlan, 'a form of Scots shaped by sea roads... On a sonic level, Shaetlan reflects its landscape; hard and open, yet with constant fluctuations of light. I like this wilderness inside it; the way it occupies a poem's heart.'

'Now let us look below the surface,' says Michael Donaghy, 'to something I find far more mysterious'. In his wonderful essay *Wallflowers*, Donaghy argues that the oral tradition is the absolute centre of gravity of all poetry, and the origin of poetic form: 'poetic rhythm precedes both our visual and auditory fields ... it's hard-wired into our brains'. And form – in poetry, in music, in dance – is the root and the starting point for innovation. Like chicks inside the egg, we humans begin to recognise sound patterns before we are born, so that from day one we are expert at recognising aural cues and patterned sound – rhythm, volume, repetition, emphasis, even rhyme and alliteration. These patterns and qualities embed us within our audience. They are what makes our language deeply performative, and deeply musical.

In poetic (i.e. innovative, creative) language, says Julia Kristeva, this 'play' with the bodily, performative qualities of speech is front-and-centre. Language, she shows,

FROM THE ARCHIVE

from *PNR* 184, vol. 35, no. 2
November – December 2008

from Hesiod's Calendar

Robert Saxton

**Contributors to the issue included
Frank Kuppner, Elaine Feinstein,
Eavan Boland and Vénus Khoury-Ghata**

To sow your seed, go naked – I'm serious.
Strip to your skin to plough, and strip to reap –
no better way to harvest Demeter's yield.

Strange though it sounds, this is no delirious
rite – it's expert practice. If you herd sheep,
be clothed; but not if your wealth's a golden field.

For more from the archive visit
www.pnreview.co.uk

PNR

---

is intrinsically a poetic system. We knowingly manipulate pattern and repetition, metaphor and metonymy, rhythm and timbre, gesture and pitch, to create new meanings or provoke 'shock' recognitions of old ones. We abide and transgress, with a wink to our audience. We stretch conventions to breaking point. The traditional aural techniques of verse, says Michael Donaghy, the mnemonics of rhyme, metre, and rhetorical schemes, are grown directly from a community's oral tradition; their performative musical qualities burn poetry deeper than prose. And, like a singer adopting a song, or a poet testing the boundaries of language, 'a player in such a tradition is expected to improvise, to "make it new", and the possibilities for expression within the prescribed forms are infinite'.

Tonight as I type this, a rush of starlings is circling the chimneys, landing every so often the roof outside my window. I hear them mimic and improvise around all the sounds of the street – curlews, doorbells, my neighbour unlocking his car. It is hard *not* to think of their racket as a thrashing-out and putting-to-bed of all that happened in the village today. A clamour of excited recognition, repetition, reformulation, corruption, dismissal.

In 2018, the old Court House building here in Arbroath was taken over for a month by an eccentric and truly revelatory exhibition. *Natural Selection* was put together by Andy Holden, a conceptual and video artist, with his father Peter, a veteran ornithologist, author and TV presenter. The bulk of the show was a recreation of an illegal cache of more than 7,000 birds' eggs that had been confiscated by the police. In the upstairs witness rooms, replica ceramic eggs spilled across shelves and floors, in boxes, trays and biscuit tins, large and small, in every subtle hue and pattern. (The actual cache was destroyed by the police.)

The exhibition examined our human-centric thinking around birds, including how we interpret behaviours such as nest-building and 'song'. Birdsong, said Peter, is a continually evolving record of place, and so it is at its heart a creative expression. The singer is constantly testing the relevance of its song against the weather, the local acoustic, the influx or absence of other birds, sub-aural sound, fluctuations in air pressure, irruptions in their territory or sensory environment. 'Its song is constantly becoming,' said Andy; 'it is a momentary record of the production of meaning, rather than a presentation of meaning-to-be-thought.'

And what might they be saying? We identify dialects, we record how songs change over distance, over time. We take a classic functionalist approach, linking these to territory, group identity, finding a mate. But how much do we ignore when we latch on to the familiar? And why do we disregard our own first response – of astonishment, that *I* should have witnessed *this* thing *here*, in *this place*. This astonishment, which precedes and frames interpretation, is the first act in all instances of noticing.

This should be our starting point when describing other species, argues zöomusicologist Hollis Taylor. Recording, whether with language or with a fancy device, is fundamentally an act of self-projection; a personal, passionate act. Using artistic gesture or rich, figurative language to describe what we see places us alongside the non-human world and draws attention to how our lived worlds overlap. This is the only ethical strategy open to us now, says Taylor. And it points to the truth that their world continues far beyond the limits of our imagination, our conceptual structures, and even our recording equipment.

A side room of *Natural Selection* was given over to small turned wood models of the sonograms of several bird calls. I tried to imagine what sort of size the models would be if they were scaled up to match the song's actual depth and reach. One November up by Loch Fleet I was rooted to the spot by the boom of a bittern, which had been blown well off course and was sending out its polite oboe notes from the far shore, almost two miles away across cold, open water. In the evening air its call rolled round the empty hills. If I could have boomed back, I would have.

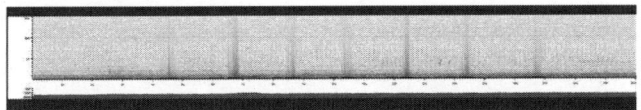

Eurasian bittern, recorded by Niels Krabbe. www.xeno-canto.com

Do birds sing?

Musicology, a discipline that originated within the classical European tradition, now encompasses interdisciplinary research into all and any musical form, expression and culture. The growing field of zöomusicology examines whether the 'musical' sounds made by other species can be truly thought of as music; that is, as an aesthetic activity, performed to some extent purely for its own intrinsic artistic value. I'm thinking of the sustained, melodic solo given by a thrush of a late-summer evening in next-door's rowan. Its joyous, overflowing stream of notes, full of exuberance and embellishment, do seem to be a singing just for the pleasure of it. But how would we know?

Composer Emily Doolittle thinks that we should reframe the question. Rather than starting with this classical definition of aesthetic activity, we should instead look for a non-human-centric common ground. Taking birdsong as an example, Doolittle identifies several outward traits it shares with human composition. Both are learned and developed in a social context in collusion with other members of the group. Both are performed for a knowing audience. In both, other singers – as a group or individually – will repeat and revise songs, creating new traditions which might in time co-exist with or come to replace the old version.

But what would the bird's definition look like? How many of their key criteria would we meet? Is exuberance and excess key to the thing? Or is their song only a song when it is sung at a certain time, in a certain light, from a certain height so that it carries out across the whole village? What would a starling say?

When we perform a dance step, a part in a play, a song, a poem, says Michael Donaghy, for that moment 'we give it a body to live in. We own a poem, or at least our expression of it in a profoundly deeper way than is possible if it is stored on a page.' A poem is 'a repository of wisdom, or wonder, or presence, if only by virtue of its own excellence. If its words are ingrained into our memories they're constantly available to our unconscious, like a computer program running in the background… they can guide us out of our emptiness.'

I wonder if there is something in the idea of place. Like a chick in the egg or a babe in the womb, we hear not just through our ears but through the bones in our head. How we form and perform language, the words we choose, our emphases and pauses, reflect the local acoustic and our instinct for how our sound will carry. Sitting here among my papers I am listening for the sounds and cadence of the lines, for hidden rhymes, and how all these things naturally fall.

These things become their own seduction. In the same way a poem suddenly finds its own form, I can imagine the blackbird singing on, long after it needs to, because the light and temperature are perfect, and the pleasure of singing, and the feel inside its body of its own song filling the world, is an ecstasy in itself.

A poetry of self-conscious listening, of placing sound carefully. Like the plover, here I am, sitting on this stone, testing out sounds and patterns in order to record how it is to be here in this now.

Weeo? Hjejle? Lo? Heilo?

Poems from Wivenhoe

MICHAEL EDWARDS

1
Drawn by hunger, hope and happiness, the congregation of villagers was time and again at the Fish and Chips. A step only, come to think of it, from the village church. The smell, up the slender by-street! No Soviet queue, a handful of locals, artists, intellectuals, the Books, perhaps, the Antiques, and housewives (if the word's still on). Greetings and head-nodding, and warm small talk, the secret bond of the English.

The shop in memory a large cubby-hole had all the trimmings, salt, vinegar, ketchup, and with them sedate on the counter a pile of ready paper. But the bonus, unique, was a further untidy pile of books left by customers and sold for pennies. Kingsley Amis in Penguins to name but him. And at our backs, as we close in on the prize, famous pargeting. What more could one ask?

And the fish! Fresh from our little port and thither from the wide and near-by at the estuary North Sea – from the Germanic Mediterranean, the English *mere ure*. Dogger, Humber, Thames, teaming with cod, rock salmon, plaice, first fried in batter by Sephardic Jews, first coupled with chips by a Jewish immigrant, popular with fish-on-Friday Catholics, created in Protestant England but not by us, a gift, and the people's choice. Hitchcock in his boyhood lived above a chippy. A miraculous catch, our survival through poverty and two World Wars.

Rambling erudition, waiting my turn, over rumbling insides.

After our gathering, each bears away his gourmet dish, this luxury. Carrying it hot back home in weather, maybe, as crisp as batter. Or, through the rain, hugging the heat burning the double wrapping against one's hands, and, arrived, thinking of the others having likewise the fish'n'chips bursting on the palate.

A modern merry-making. A little day music.

2
A strong south-easterly sun blazes and shadows the Wivenhoe streets where they run between the lines of houses like airy tunnels.

Imagination meanwhile lasers the ground for news of smugglers' bolt-holes, of the desperate and rollicking eighteenth century. The village, open to all the goodies of the Continent, lapped them up along the tidal reach, muffled some in the harbour, and stowed the contraband liquor in the huddle of taverns. ('Contraband': a word from my now underground childhood, like 'sabotage', whose mystery meant more than its meaning at the age when difficult words were pronounced slowly.) In darkness and mist, customs men and their quarry scurry with whispering feet and lanterns down the same streets, till smugglers and customers mole into the warren of tunnels. From quayside alehouse to the church – a virtuous move – goes one of these. In the jolly days of piracy, a secret society.

'Smuggling', close to snuggling, and it feels like home, having been imported from the Germanic word-hoard. What's not in a name?

The village has a hidden life, like everyone. Smuggling has to be nobler than mugging, and not only boys thrill to risk taking as heroic. The fascination of the forbidden, I muse, as I fondle a bottle snatched from legality. Set up a law and we'll break it. You can't help admiring when odds and numbers are against, when the foxy fraternity abides by strict rules, and consummate hoodwinking attains the aura of game or art. It savours of chaos transformed. Outside the law, someone breaks in, criminality hints of grace.

In the ease of a later *now*, I sipple a Polish gin brought under wraps to our surprising port by a vessel from Hamburg. We talk enviously of the deeper time beneath our own, in the street, our houses, the pubs, swapping tales of where the tunnels were and where you can still see an entrance. From time to time, when the word goes round, we pass the hot goods from one to another, quietly enjoying our underhand sociability.

3
We drive down the High Street, where I point out Max Headroom's place, with his name on the lintel. The sky is light-blue-blazer-blue, whereas story, like night, takes one into another world, or this world othered, many of Conrad's stories being tales told in darkness. Doesn't a poem also…? Indeed, in broad daylight. We meditate together, as I steer, on life, and death, and puns, our points and rejoinders lightly rocking the car, like a boat in a mild storm. It was, someone says, the 20th 'Valeria' Legion who copped this billet on the edge of the world among outlandish natives, only kept going and from revolt by regular cargoes of what was their cup of tea, real wine from home.

No longer in the palavering vehicle, we stroll through the ordered chaos of the shipyard, which passes with the casualness of a *flâneur* under our feet. The same someone remarks that, in English, boats are women except when sailing to war. Were found nearby: a neolithic arrowhead and a bronze spearhead. We do not know from whom we descend, nor how our patch of land and the sea-reach appeared through a hundred generations to other eyes. And how primitive shall we look to later? We watch a crane giddily swinging, like, say, a compass tracing an arc of air, or like, of course, a long bird-bill scanning for fish. And duck under a half-finished hull. And listen to Mauricio Kagel percussioning all around with hammers and girders and whatever comes to hand through amazing intervals and timing.

A saintly family is mentioned with a sense of comic awe as threading together the more recent ages of this Romano-Celtic, Anglo-Saxon-Norman, comical-tragical-historical village and producing as its best-known member a renowned ship-builder and smuggler. A legend falls from the air, warbling that our shipyard built a famous warship, the 'Nonesuch', for Cromwell himself, mould for Robespierre and Napoleon, for Stalin, Mao, Castro and the like, freedom sat on. As an export the Glorious Revolution flops, like English wine, there's no demand.

The sun begins to frown, from behind some clouds crept surreptitiously in. Images floating in the mind of former yachts, and frigates and freighters, and merchantmen ('These too, therefore, virile vessels'), and the sight of craft being repaired and a fair ship in the making, call up the deep and open sea, a few miles distant. We disperse, thinking of the easy walk to Brightlingsea, really quite close, where you scent, among the cries of terns and curlews, the approaching and withdrawing tide.

4
Night has returned, after a brief December day, to cover the village in its warmth. I sit writing, in a small glow, writing to no one, everyone, anyone. A horn from the river, deep in space, from time to time traverses the silence. Outside, in the narrow streets, a delicate and gleaming snow is falling. Its polar whiteness, where all the colours, invisible, meet, enriches the dark.

My wife is reading in bed. The children are asleep, their future lives, in the secret of the night, sleeping beside them. Coming lives that will slowly awake.

The day and its weight have retired. Held in this night where all things brim with reality, I find as one the burning lamp, my family safe, snow like soft diamonds, a village caressed by darkness.

The snow-capped roofs must glimmer under the tiny moon. A foreign ship glides upstream. The room, close all round, is where it is good to be, a vehicle expanding as it stirs. A night of before the beginning gathers the house, the village, the river-lands, asleep and waiting. (Not the poem but the world is threshold.) I imagine the night, penetrable darkness that reveals the stars.

How I Became a Translator

RICHARD GWYN

The title is misleading of course. It has the makings of a false narrative: *how I did this; how I did that...* as though translation were not something we are engaged in, without option and at all times, from the very start of life.

Early childhood is the acute phase of translation, and of being translated. Those moments in which every gaze, every enraged instinct on the part of the infant, meets with either incomprehension or else with a tentative, and then a more assured translation. In turn, the child who fails to translate in accordance with imposed interpretative norms will be labelled with some deficiency or syndrome that reflects inadequate life skills.

By the time we come to consider a form of translation as overt as the transference of semantic load from one language to another, we have already acquired a specific set of linguistic skills, and since a majority of children in the world grow up exposed to more than one language, decoding is a skill which has many possible applications.

Like others, I began translating in a very amateur sort of way on family holidays when confronted with signs and notices in campsites and hotels. Most particularly I was diverted by the menus in restaurants. By the time I was in my early twenties, and had abandoned Thatcher's Britain to live in Greece, I spent many frivolous hours decoding the English on restaurant menus. Among the culinary delights I encountered were:

Giant Beams
The Baked Thing
Greek with cheese
Bowel stuffed with spleen
Bait smooth hound
Mixed Peasant
Custard of the Aunt

All of these items of food have suffered the indignity of an over-literal translation by a scribe with a faulty understanding of the target language, and while their entertainment value might be high, you are never sure what it is you are likely to be eating, unless of course you can read the Greek.

Around this time I found work as a waiter in *To Diporto* (meaning 'Two Doors'), a restaurant in Hania, Crete – though no one called it that other than its Greek regulars: these were mainly conscripts from the Greek Navy, doing their thirty-six months' compulsory national service, and a smattering of local ne'er-do-wells. But by the foreign clientele of backpackers, stranded hippies on their way back from India, and US servicemen from the Sixth Fleet, harboured in Souda Bay a few kilometres down the road, the place was known as either 'The Fish Restaurant', for obvious reasons, or else 'The Pigs' Balls', which warrants a little explanation. 'Pigs' balls' was the accurate rendition of what are more delicately referred to as sweetbreads, and these were advertised, alongside other tasty specialities, on a blackboard near the front door, in English, alongside the Greek. Sweetbreads were known as τα αμελέτητα in Greek, which means, logically enough, 'the unspeakable'.

And it was within this seething hothouse of cheap food, raucous inebriation (and occasional fist fights) that my true apprenticeship as a translator took place. Michali, who was my boss (and also the chef, though to term him as such lends a dignity to his calling which he did not possess) spoke only Greek, and I had to present him with each request on an order slip, which I would take down on a small pad (a μπλοκάκι, using the pervasive Cretan diminutive). With the Greek customers, this was easy enough, and with the English speakers, I could transcribe their orders into Greek. Most of the other travellers were French or German: I spoke reasonable French, and the Germans all spoke English, so we were OK. It was the anomalies that proved most interesting – when there was no language in common and I had to improvise. But the whole exercise introduced me to some of the complexities of translation theory, and only later would I come to realise how valuable my training had been.

Since Greece was a country with which I had been a little obsessed for some years – as a teenager I had discovered a small volume entitled *Four Greek Poets* which included selections from Cavafy, Seferis, Elytis and Gatsos, in the translations of Edmund Keeley. I adored Cavafy and Seferis in particular, but only discovered the poetry of Yannis Ritsos when I started living in Crete. By then I was able to read the original Greek, and since not so much of Ritsos's work was then available in English, I thought I might have a stab at translating him myself. But my Greek proved inadequate to the task and I lacked any kind of self-discipline. I became easily disheartened by my feeble efforts and never stuck with it.

*

Some years later, I started a translation of Jean Giono's novel *Les Grands Chemins* but was put off by the quantities of unfamiliar slang and argot in the dialogue. As with most of my endeavours at that period of my life, I had an unrealistic grasp of my own abilities. With Italian I fared a little better, partly because at the time I could manage that language quite fluently, and also because the poet I was attempting to translate, Michele Ranchetti, was my first wife's uncle, and I had access to help from members of his family. I never published these poems, and a translation of Ranchetti's work appeared soon afterwards in English... but the exercise planted in me some assurances that I was gaining in understanding about what literary translation involved.

Having attempted translation from Greek, French and Italian, and been found wanting, like a serial reoffender I thought I should try my hand at Spanish. When I had acquired enough of the language to read poetry without constant referral to the dictionary, I set about translating (or should I say despoiling) Antonio Machado – a bad choice, not only because he had proven a challenge to far more experienced translators than myself, but because his Spanish is, well, utterly embedded in the thought and landscape of Castile – and I did not really appreciate or understand this at the time and concluded that perhaps I was just not very good at translating poetry. However, Machado really is more untranslatable than most, and maybe this is one of the reasons Don Paterson opted to go for much looser versions in his collection, *The Eyes*.

But with another Spanish poet, Jaime Gil de Biedma, I felt that my translations began to sing – and moreover, I could sense an affinity with this writer that extended beyond the act of translation. There were English translations of his poems available but they seemed weak to me, and I wanted to make something better, do justice to his work in a way that his American translator had not: such is the arrogance of the beginner. So I worked on a few, sent them to a magazine, and they were accepted.

I became so interested in the act of translation that I decided to put myself through the ordeal of preparing for and sitting the Institute of Linguists' 'Diploma in Translation', which at the time described itself as the 'gold standard' qualification for translators in the UK. I managed to pass the rather arduous seven hours of examination (Spanish to English), and so was legitimately able to call myself a qualified translator, even though, as with most of the achievements I have realised over the years, I also experienced a sort of scepticism or disbelief about my own alleged status. Like many people who do not admit it publicly, I thought of myself back then as an impostor for much of the working day, and for this reason the occupation of 'translator' seems a very appropriate one.

And why is this? Is there an association with the trickster, the coyote figure or the dissembler, summarised in the much-touted and increasingly irritating Italian phrase *traduttore, traditore*? A translator can make of himself another person, rather like the writer. Precisely like the writer, in fact. And as Justo Navarro observes, 'to be a writer is to turn into someone else, into a stranger. You have to begin to translate yourself. Writing is a case of impersonation, of adopting a new personality. Writing is pretending to be another.'

I also think – and clearly I am not alone in doing so – that there is something intrinsically fraudulent in the act of translation. You are trying to pretend that something is what it is not. So the trick is to make it sound as though it were not something that it is not, otherwise you end up writing translator-speak, with which we are all familiar from the study of Greek menus and furniture assembly kits.

The idea of translating into English is to make the words sound as though they were composed in English, which of course they were not, in the first instance. So we pretend, and share the pretence. If the translation is any good, then we forget we are pretending. Hence the phenomenon of reviewers praising an author's wonderful prose style, when what they are reading is in fact the prose of the translator.

The word metaphor is useful here. Translation is essentially a metaphoric process, in the sense described by Lakoff and Johnson, as 'transferring from one domain of experience to another', with the difference that the 'domain of experience' in question is another language, together with all the associated cultural baggage that goes with it. I remember being particularly impressed on discovering that the public transport system in

Athens was called METAPHORA, so that even getting a bus from A to B involves some manner of crossing from one domain of experience to another.

*

For the translator, there is often a profound satisfaction – something akin to the breaking of a code or the unravelling of a puzzle – when the correct phrase or expression slots into place, which makes translation, when it is going well, such a rewarding occupation.

Norman di Giovanni, in his essay 'A Translator's Guide', quotes Borges as saying that 'The translator is a very close reader; there is not much difference between translating and reading'. Di Giovanni finds this simple, clear approach to be in stark contrast to much of the talk and theorising about translation which takes place, he says, on a 'dizzyingly rarefied plane'.

The most helpful advice I have read on the craft of translation always keeps it simple, like Borges's remark about being a close reader: understand the source text (decode it) and put it into language as clearly as possible (encode it). Working from these clearest of principles, and with the minimum of self-deception, are the kinds of rules even an inveterate self-doubter should find easy enough to follow. Attending a workshop with the brilliant Edith Grossman, I found her emphasising the same point – to keep it simple – and that is something I have sought to follow ever since.

And yet there is more: there is a twinge of excitement, almost a sense of vertigo, closely related to the type of exhilaration experienced when one's own writing is going well (it is practically the same thing after all). Tim Parks finds this grappling with meaning to be like a constant exchange between the inchoate and the specific, between the undefined and the defined:

> Translation too is this, leaving the definition, the apparent definition, of the original, going through a state of indefinition, perhaps more original [...] than the original, where ideas are somehow held wordless, or almost, in my mind (I wish I could decide whether those ideas actually do become wordless) thence to reappear, gradually recompose themselves, from fuzz to clarity, or almost, in my own language.

So much is contained by that 'or almost'. The concept of 'almost' might be considered alongside that of 'echo' in this quotation from Walter Benjamin's famous essay: 'The translator's task consists in this: to find the intention toward the language into which the work is to be translated, on the basis of which an echo of the original can be awakened in it'. Returning to Borges and simplicity, returning to the idea of an approximation. Perhaps that is the crux of all translation: it is an expression of the almost. An inexact science, and one in which the capacity for failure is harmoniously entertained. 'We find,' wrote Roberto Bolaño in *The Savage Detectives*, 'our struggles and dreams all tangled up in the same future – and that failure is called joy.' The half-obscured image of all of humanity's glorious failures serves as a backdrop to each and every act of translation.

This is partly what attracts me – this dual reconciliation of universal failure and its associated joy, and the easy slippage between my 'own' writing (which is never entirely my own, but one set of possibilities among an infinite set of potential texts) and the act of translation. And this dualism preoccupied and tantalised me even as I realised I was the sort of writer who would also be a translator, the type who is equally at home in translation as in his or her own writing. Certainly I see myself first and foremost as a writer – the translator part is an almost invisible but essential component of the writer part – and yet I don't know, have never known, where one ends and the other begins.

Poems

DICK DAVIS

Poetries

We take it that the earliest
Was that of bard, guslar, goshan,
Who sang of heroes, which was best,
The craftiest, most outrageous man,

(Or just the one who killed the most),
Who mocked the wimps and nobodies,
And dealt in blood, and loved to boast
Of booty filched from enemies;

While ancient Eros seems intent
On juvenile androgyny
With or without coerced consent –
Boys, girls, *The Greek Anthology*.

Brutal aggression, child-abuse –
We don't approve of either, do we?
Was 'poetry', then, just an excuse?
We wouldn't be caught dead… who, me?

('Goshan' – a bard in pre-Islamic Iran, an entertainer at a feast
  who sang/recited verses praising the deeds of ancient heroes.)

Plus ça change… !

The palaces were sacked, the army fled,
Chaos prevailed, the captured king was dead –

All men were equal, there was no such thing
As landlord, peasant, underdog, or king.

It wasn't long before a new court reigned
Parading protocols it had disdained

Since power when primped and codified embraces
Minutely all it claimed that it replaces

And as the novel caliphate restored
Sasanian rites that Islam had abhorred

Napoleon's gimcrack twaddle recreated
The Bourbon court the Revolution hated.

Not knowing

I used to regret not knowing
Who my ancestors were
('Ancestors' seeming too grand a word
For their anonymous blur)

My mother's people going
Only one generation back
My father's people a mysterious
Indescribable lack

No evidence in either
For great deeds or for small,
For heroism, for evil,
For any quiddity at all

But, as I approach now
Their airy anonymity,
That I am ignorant of
The pasts that make up me

Seems only appropriate,
As hearsays become equal –
And this identity or that
Has the same sequel

The same not knowing,
The same going back
To the first mysterious
Indescribable lack.

Q and A

She asked him what exile was like; he paused
Then said, 'The thing itself can't be described,
But being asked reminds me of a picture:
In Caravaggio's painting of St. Thomas
The saint inserts a finger underneath
The lid of skin above the unhealed wound
Within his saviour's side – he needs to touch it
To be quite sure that what he's told is true.'

Yass

i.m. Yass Amir-Ebrahimi Benis

I stand behind a tree that towers above
The newly-excavated grave. From here
I hear but cannot see the rabbi who
Intones the Hebrew I don't understand
Although we all know what it has to mean.
My eyes blink for a moment and I fix
Them on the gnarled trunk's lower slopes
Where ants are scurrying inexplicably.
The coffin's lowered and the mourners grasp
The spades to shovel earth... I can't see you
But hear the clods thump on your silent coffin
And see you sitting for the first time in
My class, there at the front, blurring my view
Of all the others, as I hear you whisper
'That's me', in answer to a name I call.

In a café

I see her on the terrace
Among the families there –
The shimmer of conversation
Bright in the darkening air;

The babies passed around,
Across, from hand to hand –
Small parcels of goodwill,
Time's swaddled contraband;

The west above the river
Magenta, pink, rose-red,
The schmaltzy fiddler playing
I wish... perhaps... instead...

Wine making in my mind now
Its modicum of grace,
As evening's charcoal cancels
The outline of her face.

Translation and Relation

ZOË SKOULDING

Poetry's strangeness to the ear is what pulls me in, and it may be that it's only possible to hear poetry as itself in a language that isn't one's own, where the brain isn't skating rapidly over all the sonic qualities so that it can digest 'meaning' as quickly as possible. There's an attraction to being on the outside of a language, like the electrifying moment in which I came across Lorca's line *Verde que te quiero verde* in the thumbed pages of Penguin Modern Classics, with prose translation, while I was working in a second-hand bookshop in Norwich after university. What I was hearing in my mind's ear wasn't necessarily how the line would sound to a Spanish speaker, with its castanet rattle of consonants, but it was foreign and it was poetry and I was hooked.

I'm writing this not long after hearing that the great poet and translator Pierre Joris has died. The first two volumes of *Poems for the Millennium*, the anthologies he co-edited with Jerome Rothenberg, and which found their way into my hands in 2001, were pivotal in showing me the kind of writer I wanted to be. Voluminous and disruptive, they chart multiple paths into and out from the catalysing shock of early twentieth-century avant-gardes, reading them globally from the vantage point of plural, diverse, multilingual Americas. The translations create a sense of the English language as a mesh through which many others come into view; performance scores and concrete poems expand the limits of the poem on the page, and the anthologies as a whole suggest a way of seeing English not as a monolithic end in itself, but a stop on the way to other languages and other ways of seeing. For Joris, originally from Luxembourg, the English language had synthesized French and German, giving him a new voice that was none of the languages of his upbringing. His 'nomad poetics' suggested a means of navigating the contradictions I felt as someone originally from East Anglia, writing in English in bilingual north Wales.

Most days, I live a little of my life in Welsh, whether that's writing an email at work and checking it online to see if I've got the mutations right, or watching the dramatically mundane Welsh soap *Rownd a Rownd*, which is filmed on my street (and has even, on occasion, in my house). However, despite many lessons, as well as my having close and encouraging friends who are first-language Welsh speakers, I've not yet managed to find a voice in Welsh that doesn't dry up with the embarrassment that I can't speak it better than I do. Sometimes speaking Welsh seems like part of a civic identity and public space, so I can prepare and read an introduction at a bilingual poetry reading, as if the language belongs to the situation rather than to me. At other times, it feels like a marker for an identity that I might erase by claiming, as though I'm trying to disown the power relation of English, or a sign of intimacy and trust in a community, where the whole point of it is to be held close, like a skin scent.

Welsh speakers can also have complicated relationships with Welsh, and especially with Welsh poetry, because of the divergence between spoken and written forms, and in older generations, different routes through education. My late mother-in-law grew up Welsh-speaking but brought her sons up in English, it being the language of a supposedly bright new economic future and of her South Walian husband; only in her last days in hospital did I hear her speaking Welsh. The bilingual scene that drew me in when I moved to Bangor in the 1990s revolved around Welsh-language music and the newly-formed S4C, but it was also full of lively friction with a Welsh-speaking 'establishment' that would not have seen itself as such. At the same time as encountering Welsh, I was encountering the internalized unease that is part of its minoritized situation, and the unease became part of me before the language did. None of these things is a reason to give up learning a language that creates such a distinctive world view, for example in its tendency to weave people, things and contexts together in ways that resist the long colonial sight lines of English, but I am resigned to the possibility that it might take me the rest of my life.

Meanwhile, the language of my poetry is a somewhat conflicted English, and I write poetry because of rather than despite the conflict. Many of the poets whose work I've felt closest to have a similarly unsettled relationship with English, from Lynette Roberts, writing under the influence of Welsh, to the Canadian poet Erín Moure, whose English is inflected not only by French but the intense multilingualism of her city, Montréal. Moure's practice as a translator made me want to translate, because of her uncanny ability to enact in poetry the precarious balance between languages, and to make poetry out of that non-existent space. Thanks to EU funding, I was able in the 2000s to take part in various translation workshops with Literature Across Frontiers, in which English was used as a bridge between European languages, usually those less widely spoken. In this way, I learned to translate poetry through discussion with the author, without necessarily knowing the language I was translating from, as a kind of utopian experiment. While the translations themselves were often ephemeral, existing for a performance and then scattering, the friendships were lasting. Translation was a close reading, a pretext for conversation, and it drew us into wider poetry communities as we learned from each other. I'd done a PhD in Creative Writing, but what my European contemporaries did to learn about poetry was translate but what my European contemporaries did to learn about poetry was translate, so that the process of becoming a poet was necessarily an extension of viewpoint and voice, an accommodation of otherness.

It wasn't having a language that made me want to translate – in contrast, it was the experience of translating contemporary poetry that made me want to learn a language well enough to do it independently. Welsh did not seem to offer that possibility, because if Welsh poetry is translated into English, especially in Wales, one of its key reasons for existing is liable to dissolve (there are exceptions, as for example Minhinnick's anthology *The Adulterer's Tongue*, which both respects and explains Welsh poets' resistance to English translation). Instead, I turned to French, which I'd learned as an au pair in Belgium in the 1980s but had largely forgotten. Initially, the world of French poetry seemed austere and forbidding. Then, at a poetry festival in Nicaragua in 2010, I met a Luxembourgish poet of Italian origin, Jean Portante, who was an old friend of Pierre Joris and similarly at home in several languages. While Joris had chosen English, Portante had chosen to write in French, even though Italian was his mother tongue, and it was this outside, in-between quality of his French that drew me to his work. His description of how his poetry breathed in French with an Italian lung, like the mammalian lung of a whale in its ocean life, seemed to resonate with the fish-out-of-water incongruities of my own writing. I started translating a few poems at first, then a sequence, then a book, relearning the language as I went along. Since then, French has gradually become a language I can not only translate from, but also think, feel and write in, not perfectly, but enough for it to shape a different perspective and way of being.

French has, in turn, opened up Spanish for me, which I can read and speak with varying degrees of fluency depending on the situation. The translations of my poems by Víctor Rodríguez Núñez and Katherine M. Hedeen, which have taken me to many Latin American countries, feel very much like mine, but they also feel somehow warmer than they do in English. More than that, translation creates its own geopolitical and cultural coordinates, as Hedeen and I suggest in our anthology *Poetry's Geographies: A Transatlantic Anthology of Translations*, in which we explore the work of the poet-translator in connecting and counter-mapping between poetic and political realities. In the current moment of disintegration and wilful destruction, relations between languages, positions, viewpoints, bodies and voices have never been so critical. These relations are central to what poetry is and what it does.

Poems

NELL PRINCE

From 'Baroque Fountains'

GREEK FOUNTAIN FOR A TYRANT
A culvert is equal to a polis. Peisistratus saw with clarity this wisdom. His Athenian aqueduct bent to the fountain of Enneakrounos so freshness was constantly falling in the agora, the nine beautiful spouts rushing into urns, onto bodies flocking for water.

RUNNY HARMONY
You see I should have seen it, lucid as the actual stream: *runny harmony*, running with the sun. The circling swifts understand this. This curtain of Pope's frippery has stalled the entire afternoon.

MEDITATION
Silence is a dangerous fountain revealing what was always there all along: birdsong. At last the last language out of the desert free from this static mind.

The Silence of the Setting Sun

Upon this raw October day
I have let slip a crinkled leaf.
I have bent double with the wind
and felt the rain beyond belief.
And I have watched the thunder come
across the meadow and the field
and known the answer to the drum
and shivered at its freakish light.
And I have felt my weightless crown
dull from gold to torpid brown.
I have sung with scattered wings
before the silence of the storm.
I have known the worst of ice,
the danger of its dagger form,
and I have held the thickest snow,
the wicked spell-work from the north.
And in the spring I shall put forth
a green so young you'd call it light.
And I will know the April dark,
the blossom and the April night.
I will creak and hold the lark
and hear its spotless morning song,
and I will know before too long
the silence of the setting sun.

The Desert

The desert, as you said, is partly gust,
is ghost, and also stranger than you think.
Its load of sand, roads of luxurious dust
are merely in this moment words to drink.

Its space and time make up a shady cast –
and I can tell you coming from the brink
there's nothing in the wind that's ever just,
and only gods of violence here to thank.

The desert, of course, is history. Past.
It does not, and will not ever shrink.
But then history was never meant to last,
except when tortured into page and ink.

Its endlessness you cannot know or trust,
equating to this fact: that love and life don't link.
Recall this region is just psychic crust,
that you and I are merely words to drink.

Bloody Cicero!

Cicero! Bloody Cicero, how I love my Cicero.
Always getting his hands dirty in the Senate.
Digger! Braggadocio! Brother I like to contemplate.
Cicero, I'm sitting on the moon. I am here refreshing a vision, thinking on the joined up lights of cities. Thinking again of home, and a leafy suburb, thinking of Chaucer Road where my distant Atticus never talked of poets, but talked of everything else: maths, algebra, the politeness of the Japanese, and Frankl. I am thinking of Atticus and when we walked, talked through Hyde Park, laughed at dramatic crows. Sitting on the moon like this, time has no particular face. I am shocked by my disinterest.

My mother kept me alive

please explain the things I can't discuss
I must tell you about the time
as if it mattered as if anyone had time
you know you can't kill a distance like this
I, having received treatment,
I, what a disordered
gosh and the ash of you that blows
that I wandered into the labyrinth of loss
that I must trust that I have been
on this earth I can say I can say it
my mother kept me alive

Notes from a Native

MARY O'MALLEY

To come from Connemara is to learn early, as Joan Didion so aptly put it of California, a lesson in cognitive dissonance. It is also a lesson in duality. The place I grew up in is both stark and beautiful, yet away from it, I am never nostalgic. I carry it with me like a state of grace and darkness. I know where my compass points when at rest, a spot near Slyne Head, an island covered by gold-coloured lichen, with a small sandy beach below a chapel.

My earliest picture of the world resembled Flann O'Brien's map of the world in *An Béal Bocht*, a joyous send-up of Dublin Gaelgóirí as well as *An tOileánach*, a book he greatly admired. The map depicts the world from the viewpoint of the West Kerry Gaeltacht. There are poitín deposits marked with an X as if they were oilwells, and particular prominence is given to Sligo gaol. A large landmass called 'Overseas' has three cities, New York, Boston and Springfield Mass. There are money order offices for sending dollars home, and a few longhorned cattle. England, entitled 'De Odar Saighd', has fewer money order offices and contains George Bernard Shaw. China is close to America, and the legendary Tír Faoi Thoinn, the land under the sea, is marked by a pair of legs sticking up out of the water between these two unlikely coasts.

My own world, at about four or five years old, looked roughly like this: Slyne Head, the Twelve Bens, Errislanann, Carna, Caillín's Well, Pittsburgh Pennsylvania, where my Aunt was. When I was shown it on an atlas with the states of America marked out in different colours, I wanted to eat Pennsylvania. Spain, Valparaíso and California came from the songs, and I found The Missions, which included the Far East, in the religious magazines I leafed through before I went to school. Then there was Dublin, which was where you went to get the visa. My territory expanded when I learned to read, but before that, there was Boston and Broadway, which was connected to The Old Bog Road. Young as I was, I remember wondering why anyone would want to leave Broadway for the bog. England featured in a vague sort of way.

I learned to read reasonably early. The world I entered through books was a kind of reversal of Miles na gCopaleen's map, a world that moved out from Dublin and London and came West for poverty and Playboys. Since then, quite a bit has been written about somewhere called Connemara. Its place names have been parsed, its bungalows scorned, its scenery depicted as stark, dramatic, beautiful. Its coast has been praised, as if it had earned itself a PhD in Beauty and Wildness through hard work and noble savagery. It is wild, lovely and, depending on what you read, half ruined or half preserved. In the 1980s, some even claimed that it was undiscovered, with the logic of a child who covers his eyes and believes himself invisible, but all are agreed that preserving this Shangri La matters. This Connemara sounds beautiful. It is popular, and important for the people who holiday there, for the environment and giant windmills and for those who generally feel its beauty is good for the soul, if the soul can still be mentioned in polite company. On paper it mostly sounds distant and empty, except for a few intrepid thrill-seeking adventurers and the occasional local, almost always a 'guide' or a 'fisherman' or a 'character'. The coast is rugged, the Atlantic prone to swells and the prose tends towards hyperbole. It sounds vaguely familiar but I have never been there.

Its savagery, its beauty, its overblown gestures and simple or sly inhabitants have been described in glimpses and served up in anecdotes. It is a land of brown bread and potatoes and dolphins, written about by travel writers and proselytizers, most of them with admiration. Shibbolets, seafóid, half-truths, truths – it's all in there among the thatched cottages and dreams of well-meaning tourists and colonisers. But where is the place I know? In the stories and the songs, the sean-nos and the dancing certainly, but perhaps above all else, it is in the sea. Its rhythms and sounds set up a cadence that has never left me and that corresponds to the essence of the place I was born into.

Let me start again. If a story can have more than one ending, surely it can have more than one beginning. In a poet's case, it is the beginning that changes – we know the ending but the start is not always as it first seemed.

I grew up in Errismore. When I looked for our place in books it was not to be found. Villages and townlands were mentioned, slightly misplaced, like shadow images mislaid over real pictures. It was foreign, in those books, from a map, not a chart. The landmarks were familiar, but they were placed in a flattened country, like those paintings of Tory Island seen from the seagull's voracious point of view. It is a natural impulse, to remake a place in the image of what you know, to frame its narrative from your own starting point. Shakespeare's magical island in *The Tempest* was in many ways 'forever England' and Caliban, the only local, got the villain's part. At least he got a part, and a dominant one at that.

You could read a shelf of books on 'Connemara' in English, with the exception of Richard Murphy's poems and Tim Robinson's essays and maps, and John M. Synge's remarkably unromantic reports for the *Manchester Guardian*, and know nothing of the place itself. What was missing, in part, was language, and with it, a point of view and a way of life, what we call 'culture'.

I first encountered my own world in the stories of Liam Ó Flaithearta and Máirtín Ó Cadhain. Every rock was familiar and the sea in all its capricious moods, though not one was set in Aillebrack or Errislanann. I found my place in the poetry of Máirtín Ó Direáin, and in *Dialann*

Deoraí by Dónall Mac Amhlaigh, a Galway man who went to Scoil Fhursa National school, where both my own children would go many years later. I found the life I knew, in short, in Irish; and off the page, I already knew it in songs and music, the songs mostly, though not all, in English. I believe Borges is right when he says that 'in music, form and substance cannot be torn asunder'.

'Gaelic', Yeats said, 'is my national language but it is not my mother tongue.' Irish is my mother tongue but I was raised in English. I grew up on the Errismore peninsula. My mother came from the next peninsula, Errislannan. She was born a mile from where Alcock and Brown made their famous landing, cushioned by boggy land after their pioneering crossing from Newfoundland. Within a short distance, in Derrigimla, Marconi set up one of his stations in 1907. On another peninsula, to the south, my maternal grandmother was born near Rosmuc, a few miles from where the writer Pádraic Ó Conaire stayed with his uncle and learned to speak Irish as the locals spoke it. As you make your way from one of those houses to the other, direction changes. Place is not tethered reliably to location – it all depends on where you start out from. In the past, the reliable roads, and by far the shortest, were by sea.

Irish mythology, with its islands that appear and disappear, its 'Ceo Draoichta' and 'Tir na nÓg', was not predicated on a world nailed down. Our places existed in language as much as in space. The entire Táin is dedicated to naming places. It is topographically accurate; you can still trace the route of the great cattle raid. The Morrigan's Cave is reached through a slit in a field in Co. Roscommon, narrow as a birth canal. Cruachan Ai, the great earthworks associated with Maeve, is recognisable still, as long as you are not expecting palaces. The Cooley peninsula, site of the great cattle raid, is famous for, and in part because of, its music. Ulster is still reliably Ulster but of the five original provinces which gave us the word 'cúige', a fifth, only four remain. The fifth has long since disappeared in terms of mapping, yet it never left the language or the imagination, as if its absence in itself focused attention on the need for re-invention. A space, according to Mark Hederman 'which is neither physical, geographical, nor political. It is a place which is beyond or behind the reach or our normal scientific consciousness.'

I know every rock and field at home but my grandmother's house was sold to cement merchants. Holiday homes, often referred to as cottages by their owners, replaced the houses I knew. I lived in Errismore, which has all but disappeared. Now a whole set of people inhabit a quantum reality called Connemara, obliterating names and distinctions 'in a well-meaning act of recolonization. Whole areas are called Roundstone, or Ballyconneely, as if there were no villages, no named fields. Such is the reality of tourism. An invented identity is imposed over a place, impervious to its music and its real presence. A clever slogan becomes a reality as place becomes a marketplace. There is nothing new in this, nor is it unique to Ireland, nor to Connemara/Conamara, but it is important to me because it was my home.

In his essay entitled 'The Placeless Heaven', Seamus Heaney credits Patrick Kavanagh for allowing him to 'dwell without cultural anxiety among the usual landmarks of your life'. The poets that did that for me were Ó Direáin and Ó Flaithearta, Máire Mhac an tSaoi, and, later, Caitlín Maude and Michael Hartnett. That I would have more in common poetically with Derek Walcott, Pablo Neruda and Octavio Paz than with either Ó Direáin or Ó Flaithearta mattered not at all. Only they could reflect my own place back to me in its own words. Only in their work could I find that permission. They allowed me to stand on the rock I belonged on, and move out. Out to other countries and their literature, and to the freedom and discovery of new languages and different cadences and forms.

The contradiction at the heart of this situation is that I couldn't write in the language that was, in effect, my mother tongue. I couldn't write in it because of a lack of fluency, and a certain rigour in my own approach that, rightly or wrongly, I feel is crucial to poetry. My Irish is not, and was not, good enough because I grew up mostly through the medium of English. My English was not good enough either and I was unsure of it, but it was in that language, for the most part, that I got my education. Of course, I have written poems in Irish, but not with the full deck at my disposal. What has all this to do with place? Well, as Heaney found in Kavanagh 'a poetry which linked the small farm life which produced us with the slim volume world we were now supposed to be fit for', I found in Ó Direáin and Ó Flaithearta the place and the life I knew, and the place was permeable to the life of the people as they were permeable to the hills and strand and rocks.

When people left Connemara, which they did in droves, they took the place with them. One man, Séamus Mac an Iomaire, wrote *Cladaí Chonamara*, an invaluable guide to the shore life of his area, while confined to bed in New York. The emigrants took Connemara with them in songs, in music, in poems and in the soles of their feet. That there was a deep tectonic contradiction between this Conamara and the Connemara out of which the poet must somehow work, I accept on the level of the mind. The deeper self knows that somewhere in that early chasm, in the attraction of a rock in the Atlantic called 'Carraig Scoilte', or 'Split Rock', is a truth that needs little explanation. Certain words, Borges believed, have meaning not for reason but for the imagination. Or for the imagination first, and reason lags behind. Borges also believed that a nation evolves the words it needs, and so we kept certain words in Irish – not because we didn't know the other words but because the English equivalent wasn't what we meant – among them sceach, liabhán, and gleoiteog. Three of those words are central to three of the poems in my latest collection, *The Shark Nursery*. The poems are in English, but the images that anchor the bright blossoms of the thorn bush to Eavan Boland's shade, to the basking sharks guarding their territory, to Josie Sheáin Jeaic Mac Donncha's coded songs or the sails being raised on a boat in the Claddagh Basin after lockdown, are sceach geal, liabhán gréine and gleoiteog.

Saving Civilisation

Stefan Collini, *Literature and Learning: A History of English Studies in Britain* (Oxford), £35

TONY ROBERTS

'The "teaching of literature" has planted a terrible fixed foot in our schools and colleges.' – George Saintsbury, *Matthew Arnold* (1899)

In a December 2022 issue of the *London Review of Books*, Stefan Collini began an admiring review of John Guillory's *Professing Criticism* with the admission that when he explained his own work-in-progress, the idea 'seems to strike many people as at once unrealistically ambitious and largely pointless'. When he further explained that it was not a history of criticism but an institutional history, 'the bafflement turns to boredom and the silent reflection that it takes all sorts'. Now we have *Literature and Learning*, the result of *his* perceived need (and ten years of study): an excellent and comprehensive treatment of the history of Literature in mainstream education in Britain from the 1860s to the 1960s.

Collini is Emeritus Professor of Intellectual History and English Literature at Cambridge University and one of our best writers: a meticulous and stylish authority on nineteenth and twentieth-century ideas. Latterly he has also emerged as a highly regarded polemicist in defence of British universities. When asked about his *What Are Universities For?* (2012), he said in interview that 'one of the most pressing immediate needs seemed to me to be to help academics maintain a bit of self-belief' in the face of political and media criticism. And in *Speaking of Universities* (2017), he defended these institutions against perceived public indifference and the rampant market values swallowing academic ones, within a great 'financialization' of higher education.

In *Literature and Learning* what has really interested him is how, over his chosen period, '"Eng Lit" slowly gained cultural and institutional primacy in England'. It is something of a departure for him, as he acknowledges, since here he is tracing the history of educational institutions with a 'commitment to plenitude of empirical detail' running to 648 pages. The detail he sees as required because the subject has hitherto received only fitful and incomplete attention.

Collini bases his evidence on a variety of institutional records, on education reports and acts and on contributions from the historical participants. His method is to avoid the seeming seamlessness of an 'unbroken linear narrative approach'. Instead his thematic account 'involves the interweaving' of several histories: the idea of English literature and its standing in cultural terms; the history of literary scholarship and criticism (as distinct from 'lay' literary culture); and the history of universities and their disciplines. Interesting questions are addressed throughout: how Literature overcame the obstacle of its putative subjectivity; how it avoided being subsumed within History or Languages; how it asserted itself against the Classical and philological elements; and how Scottish education influenced English studies.

Collini is careful to avoid promoting misconceptions. He makes it clear, for example, that in the early days of English and Scottish higher education numbers were very low and courses rudimentary (given the younger age of entrants). There were no more than a thousand students in Scotland in 1700, and the University of Durham (founded in 1832) had fewer than a hundred, with no full English course until the twentieth century. Also, 'English language and literature' courses involved other areas of study, and Literature itself for many years meant the history and appreciation of poetry.

Organizational changes created a more recognizably modern system of education with the founding of the secular University of London in 1836, from 1858 an examining body not restricted to the two London colleges (King's and University College). This influenced school syllabuses and promoted English Studies, as did Oxbridge local examinations from 1858 and those for entrance to the burgeoning Indian Civil Service.

From the mid-nineteenth century, the teaching of English literature tended to involve rhetoric, German-influenced philology, appreciative criticism (belletrism) and literary history (seen, in Henry Morley's words, as 'the story of the English mind'). The rhetorical tradition lasted longest in Scotland. Philology, thought to bring the necessary rigour of the sciences to Literature, eventually began to lose its 'scholarly prestige', for 'it served wider pedagogical purposes poorly, tended to be unattractive to students, and had only a limited application to post-medieval literature' (English being heavily dependent on Anglo-Saxon study). After the First World War, it was also tarred with its heavy German influence.

The importance of the Classics, which historically appealed to the 'governing elite', had been the subject of discussion for the century that Collini's book covers, though even in this period its almost total dominance of the curriculum was being undermined, so that that by 1868, 43 percent of old endowed grammar schools taught neither Latin nor Greek. It took nearly another century for Greek to all but disappear and for Latin O-level to be dropped as an entry requirement at Oxbridge. Ultimately it was as difficult to argue that Latin drill matched its ideals as that literature necessarily delivered a moral education.

Collini reports on the establishment of provincial universities after Durham – Manchester, Liverpool and Leeds, followed by Birmingham, Sheffield and Bristol in the new century – and on university extension education, especially in Literature, which became popular from mid-century. His treatment of Literature at Oxbridge is more detailed and character-driven, since what happened in these institutions had 'disproportional influence' around the country and was the subject of debate in *The Times* and in periodicals like the *Pall Mall Gazette*. Until English studies became recognized there, it was unlikely to be granted discipline status.

One necessary theme in *Literature and Learning* is the woeful provision of educational opportunities for women. The lack of training offered girls in the Classics and in science meant they could not compete with men at the highest levels even where opportunity arose. The Taunton Commission of 1869 found only fourteen endowed secondary schools for girls in England (572 for boys) and it was not until the 1902 Balfour Education Act, which created LEAs, that educational provision for girls was improved.

However, by mid-nineteenth century public interest stirred. In 1849 the Ladies College in Bedford Square was founded and in 1878 the University of London admitted women to examinations. While women's colleges were opened in cities like Bristol, Manchester and London, it took until 1920 at Oxford (and 1948 at Cambridge) that women were entitled to study for degrees. And yet by 1930 women made up 27 percent of the student population in Great Britain. They were overwhelmingly found in the Arts faculties and particularly in English. Collini traces these developments and then turns to the careers of three chair-holding scholars: Caroline Spurgeon, the first female professor at an English University (author of *Shakespeare's Imagery*), Edith Morley and Bertha Phillpotts.

As Collini is careful to restrict his focus to the contribution of individuals to the rise of Literature, he marginalises some eminent names of the period. So Matthew Arnold, on whom Collini is an authority, is given limited attention. While indefatigable in support of education, Arnold remained intoxicated by Classicism, having little interest in university Literature as an independent subject. Instead Collini reflects on other Victorian and modernist educators who achieved prominence when tenure advanced the attraction of a career in university teaching. He first singles out three noted English professors who at one time held chairs in Scottish universities: A.C. Bradley, Walter Raleigh and George Saintsbury.

It was the popular Bradley who, at the prospect of serving as Oxford Professor of Poetry, wrote candidly: 'I feel as if I had no message about literature and as if all the talk about it were mere voluptuousness'. To Collini, he is a key figure, comparable to Arnold: 'He articulated an understanding of literary value that came nearer than the work of any of his contemporaries to providing a rationale for much of the pedagogical and scholarly practice of the middle decades of the twentieth century.' And his *Shakespearean Tragedy*, perhaps because it was aimed at a wide audience, remains a text in play.

'There is no escaping Saintsbury', Collini writes of the ardent Tory classicist, citing a massive publishing history. Saintsbury was the most famous critic of his day, his *A Short History of English Literature* (1898) apparently running to 800 pages. He was foremost a reviewer and a writer of histories and surveys, as well as a popular if rambling lecturer. (According to John Gross, in *The Rise and Fall of the Man of Letters* (1969), a former student recalls learning a specimen sentence by heart: 'But while none, save these, of men living, had done, or could have done, such things, there was much here which – whether either could have done it or not – neither had done'). As with most critics of the time, Saintsbury's 'relaxed, discursive' method fell out of favour when the assumptions about the 'rich and stable literary tradition' changed.

Walter Raleigh and Sir Arthur Quiller-Couch are twinned by the similarity of their academic backgrounds, their devotion to literature and by the dash they had about them. Raleigh escaped to Oxford, where he was expected to give a quarter of the lectures required at Glasgow, and where he set about building a school of English. He earned admiration for his lecturing and administrative efforts (being knighted in 1911) rather than for his published work. Quiller-Couch, a man of letters and political Liberal with an interest in all three educational tiers, gave celebrated lectures on Literature to large numbers (800 in London, with many turned away). While both triumphed in their time, Raleigh's influence at Oxford declined later, while 'Q's' flourished at Cambridge.

Collini also writes of John Churton Collins, a fierce advocate of English Literature, and of John Bailey, not an academic but a critic and conservative man of letters, who worked for the English Association and the Newbolt Committee. Other recognizable and colourful figures, such as Leslie Stephen and William Empson, are marginal to Collini's focus, and other big names – T.S. Eliot, I.A. Richards and F.R. Leavis – are judged not to be quite as central to the institutional Literature of their day, however transformative their views might later have become to parts of the discipline.

Eliot flirted with university teaching, while always ambivalent about university scholarship and even the teaching of literature: 'Viewed from the perspective of the years when Eliot was most critically active and creative (roughly 1917–23), the relation of his work to the study of literature in universities seems more uncertain, less teleological, and in some ways more puzzling.' Richards's direct involvement in university policy-making was limited and his real interest lay beyond the discipline, in 'theoretical enquiries in communication'. His famous *Practical Criticism* acted, popularly, as an exposé of the limits of student understanding of poetry as much as an encouragement to close reading skills.

Of Leavis, Collini writes: 'The heart of Leavis's paradoxical relation to the development of the discipline lies in the fact that his scorn for the academicism and alleged intellectual nullity of the established practices of literary history and philology was matched by a soaring ambition to make the proper teaching of English in a university not just a uniquely ramifying discipline there, but the one hope of saving civilization from the destructive forces of its own materialism and inattention.' His influence and the influence of *Scrutiny* proved greater outside Cambridge, where acolytes took university posts. Collini concedes, 'Leavis brought a personal urgency to the activity of studying literature'.

Terry Eagleton, a critic with whom Collini is happy to contend (as he does in the useful bibliographical essay at the book's end), noted recently, in *Critical Revolutionaries*, that 'Cambridge English' was 'a marginal, minority affair'. Here Collini explores the 'myth', concluding that 'only after 1945, and more visibly still in the 1950s, did [the new critical manner] become widespread in the study and teaching of English literature in British universities'. He also points out that it involved more than 'practical criticism' alone and that the methodology had antecedents in earlier practice at Cambridge.

In paying more attention to specific educational figures I am conscious of limiting the scope of *Literature and Learning*. For instance, Collini looks in detail at the organisation of English in various university departments, taken from the work of *Critical Survey* (1963–6). He also discusses the growth of educational publishing, and the rise of educational journals such as the *Review of English Studies* (1925) and the later *Critical Quarterly*, as well as the role of the *English Association* and the *Newbolt Report* on English teaching in England (1921).

Chris Baldick, writing in *The Social Mission of English Criticism, 1848 to 1932* (1983), noted 'a growing "opposition" movement', 'which has begun to question some of the long-standing assumptions of traditional literary criticism'. In his final chapter, 'Doubts', Collini locates this unsettling of Literature from the end of the sixties, when 'many more voices were to be heard questioning this confidence in the current state of literary studies, voices that challenged the assumptions about "literature" that underwrote it and the understanding of "criticism" that animated its practice'. In a decade or so, his 'many voices' had become 'a movement'.

At one point in his book Collini quotes Dr Johnson's comment on *Paradise Lost*: 'None ever wished it longer than it is'. The churlish could say the same here. And yet, as a thorough workout of its subject, *Literature and Learning* is a necessary contribution to the study of Literature in British educational history and one accomplished with characteristic erudition and energy.

Two Poems

DAN BURT

Melamed

I

He stole into the classroom first day of term
a slight stooped shadow from the Pale
to train pre-teen boys to chant
verses from Old Testament tales
in Hebrew consonants and vowels
they didn't understand or care to learn.
His wrinkled polyester drip-dry
navy-blue suit and tie
washed-out white shirt with ravelled thread
black kippah too small for his bald head
and *Haftorot*[1] spilling from his satchel
announced '*yeshiva bocher*[2] from dead shtetl'.

II

Origins meant nothing
to the wanton youths he faced
racketing in tablet-chairs arrayed
before a table serving as his desk:
Yeledim,[3] *please.* (They ignore the precative.)
Yeledim! (His tremelo guts the imperative.)
Hostile, brazen they take his measure
like wolves prowl a wounded hart
mark the shaking hands, his start
at a slammed door or peal of thunder
the lowered eyes that evade their gaze –
a beaten beast, cowed, castrate.

---

1 Selections from the Books of the Prophets, passages from which Jewish boys chant before the synagogue congregation when they are called to the Torah as part of their Bar Mitzvah ritual.
2 Orthodox Jewish males who devote their lives to studying the Torah to the exclusion of all else.
3 *Boys* in Hebrew.

III

They vie to spook him all *cheder*[4] year
lured by sour odour of his latent fear –
crash! They upset a chair; *blam!*
a cherry-bomb goes off in a trash can –
and snigger when he freezes or cowers
as if a bell tolled his final hour.
Too young and feral to seek the root
of tremors and panics that made him their butt
they blame too much davening or parsing Kashrut[5]
and smear him with slurs goys shout at them
shamed by his frailty, his role as their goat
that they share his race, shoulder same yoke.

IV

The sweaty somnolence of a June afternoon
at the end of his year teaching them to be Jews
drove the melamed to doff suit-coat
and roll cuffs which debuted as they rose
five fading digits between left elbow and wrist
tattooed when his transport emptied at Auschwitz.
'I am a survivor' the stigmata say
'my fear the gash slave-labour made
that ignorant urchins from privileged cots
poke, gouge and piss on for their sport
faces afire with the same delight
I first saw in a *Deutschland Meister's*[6] eye.'

We played on, none spared a tear.
Mr Kushner did not return next year.

Palimpsest

(for Rufus)

I

No diner here wore denim
overalls to kindergarten
that weekly washings and Delta toil
scrubbed pewter-blue and gossamer
except the man whose guests we are.
His line-backer bulk in asphalt-grey
12-ounce wool Brooks Brothers suit
cerulean Sea Island shirt
and four in hand scarlet silk tie,
his glistening bald hemisphere
atop a horseshoe ear to ear
of nubby sexagenarian silver hair
promise competence summoning
  champagne
four courses, claret, port
in this K Street[7] power-brokers' haunt.
Only melanin sets him apart
from other hosts in this restaurant.

---

4 Hebrew primary school teaching basics of Judaism and Hebrew language.
5 Jewish dietary laws argued about incessantly by Talmud students.
6 'Der Tod ist ein Meister aus Deutschland' (Death is a Master from Germany) 'Todesfuge', Paul Celan.
7 DC's main street for lobbyists' offices and expense account restaurants.

II

Nothing hinted at cotton rows
and shot-gun shacks by red clay roads
where he'd been minted
nor five-decade anabasis through
Jim Crow schools, HBCU[8]
and hay-seed university law degree
to lead lobbyist at PG&E
in the Capital.[9] The waiter ignores his eye
and lays the tab down by my side,
the young, sole white male at our table.

'I'm paying, not him. Bring it to me.'
'Oh... excuse me, I thought...'
'What?'
'uhh, well, uh, um, er....'
Carotids bulging, on his feet
'What? What did you think?'
through bared teeth.
We knew what he thought.

III

Sixty years of signs down-home
on toilets, fountains, waiting rooms –
No Coloureds, *Whites Only* –
police, officials all the colour of bone
still called *Boy* when fully grown,
in diapers schooled to suffer sleights
in silence, hide pride and indignation's trace –
Don't sass. Walk by.
Cross the street. Know your place. –
reflexively draw rein, tuck chin
automatically avert his face
scrape fury's lineaments away
and over a lifetime's palimpsest of rage
repaint the mask of a facilitator
he wears in C-suite and Capitol corridor.

We leave in silence, politely part apace
never again mention
how I watched a nation's id
shame a paragon and race.

Turning Back: The Poetry of Claire Malroux

JENA SCHMITT

Daybreak: New and Selected Poems, Claire Malroux (NYRB Poets, 2020), £13.99

To read Claire Malroux's *Daybreak: New and Selected Poems*, translated from the Marilyn Hacker, is to wander contentedly around an art-filled museum for the day. Imagine seeing Matisse's *Intérieur aux aubergines*, its blue-flowered wallpaper and wavering red tablecloth next to the phosphorescent-green dining-room doorways of Wassily Kandinsky's *Interieur (Mein Esszimmer)* and Harriet Backer's glowing studio, *Mitt atelier*. Down a quick corridor and into another gallery: Monet's poppy-filled *Coquelicots*; Sonia Delaunay's abstract sunrise in *Simultaneous Contrasts*; Gabriele Münter's bright-yellow house, *Stillleben vor dem gelben Haus*, behind a still life of oranges and pink begonias.

Let's walk into another room – I mean, poem – this time by Malroux:

The entryway blazes
buttercup-yellow bamboo furniture
radiant on stiff, spindly legs
garnished with even brighter flowered cushions
or ones whose fluid egg-yolk satin
bursts from beneath the crust
of dun-coloured crochet-work
images of the sun

---

8   Historically Black Colleges and Universities.
9   Pacific Gas & Electric, one of America's largest regulated natural gas and electric power companies, with 16 million customers.

Next to this:

> but beyond that entry opens out
> the twilit dining room, smoke-hued curtains
> on a wooden rod, a hanging fixture with three
>   tulip globes
> dappled blue...

And then this:

> Huge purple flowers spring from black corollas
> We hardly ever go into that room
> whose north window looks out on the road

Malroux's poems are as bright as paintings. Not only picturesque but ekphrastic in the Ancient Greek sense of the word: vivid descriptions that bring the subject right before the reader's eyes. Poems are adorned with 'lime-green chestnuts', 'William Morris peacock blue', the wispy amethyst of 'wisteria on a wrought-iron door', a dress 'with azure polkadots'. And in her parents' kitchen, these exquisite details feel as alive today as when Malroux was a child:

> From a cloth mat on the shelf droop scallops
> printed with red cherries
> and on the graduated ceramic storage jars
> a checkerboard pattern
> alternates blue-violet and white squares
> where fruits also nestle, curled in leaves

It is easy to envision what Malroux means, for she's done the meticulous work of finding words to describe the spaces she inhabited – and continues to inhabit – in combinations of colour, texture, pattern, sound. Even death has a taste: like cake. The rhythm of her lines reflects this careful acquisitioning – methodical, lilting, step-like. Reading her poems, one could imagine walking around these rooms – here is a table with clawed feet, there, a cloisonné bowl – seeing everything she sees.

'Observation plays a great part in my work', she says. So, too, remembering. The two go hand in hand, where the past presents itself firmly in the present: her parents and sister sitting at the kitchen table; German soldiers marching past her Paris window; her grandmother worrying about feeding her family; friends' voices like ringing bells in the city square; her father's time in the Résistance, the dreaded knock at the door that leads to his death at Bergen-Belsen.

The impressionistic remains of a then-as-now scenery scroll by:

> At the crest, the cemetery, a citadel
> wrapped round by cypress and yew
> sheltering within its high white wall
> phantoms beneath iron crosses
> and bizarrely tortured mauve enamel flowers
> a foreign city
> at the border
> beyond the ditch teeming with tadpoles.

Scenes like these have a sweeping episodic effect. 'The episode is brief / The door closes again', but Malroux is quick. She captures memories, or perhaps memories of memories – each remembrance an act of remembering. Caught, *click*, as though in a photograph. Or, as Malroux writes, 'An explosion amongst the millions / Of memory's bombardments...'. Every so often, she breaks through memory's – and perhaps writing's – artifice: 'the screen tears open / So we can touch them'.

In Malroux's poems, cataclysmic events such as war and the loss of a parent or loved one permanently alter one's physical and emotional landscapes. From the 'bullet-pocked facades' to '[s]hattered bricks, flayed sockets / Facing the snow's glare of absence', there are more stark observations:

> Annihilated garden, statue with feet of clay
> Although anchored in earth   To anchor it within
> Yourself Would be a trap   Paradises only last
> When lost   Bury it in your own depths instead
> The fir tree upside down to seize
> The soil's surging, the bushes hollowed

In the second, third and fourth lines in the poem above, Malroux forges through, forgoing punctuation mid-line. In another poem, a sudden, clipped 'Our eyes Our blank Our anguish' not only speeds up but heightens the despair. No time to take a breath or look in another direction. No time to stop – the line implies – keep going. After leaves choke the narrator's throat – '*Victory, defeat, are unimportant*' – she writes, 'The new Dark Ages are announced / Which will not be tamed by metaphors'. Poetry, for Malroux, is another battle, which she describes in an interview in Paris with Gabriella Ricciardi for *Women in French Studies* (1999):

> *Je conçois la poésie un peu comme une espèce de guerre, de lutte permanente... C'est une tentative toujours couronnée d'insuccès, parce qu'il est évident que jamais on n'arrive à atteindre l'insaisissable...*

> [I see poetry a bit as a kind of war, a permanent struggle... It is an attempt always crowned with failure, because it is obvious that we can never succeed in reaching the elusive...]

And yet, through poetry, Malroux reveals how hauntingly cruel history – and historic recurrences – can be. In the news, one can still read something like this:

> they're at the dark heart of the crisis
> Aerial attacks take them by surprise
> in the midst of their homework
> which they finish underground in the shelters

And this:

> War has changed people's habits
> Transportation is difficult
> they stay home

> Close friends have died, are dying
> The current of life
> Bypasses the emptied house's island

And even more precisely here: 'How are the little ones, my grandmother asks / They're fine, but they don't have enough to eat'. These sentiments reveal the accuracy and candour of Malroux's perceptions, her sensitivity to the spaces around her, the experiences she moves through: 'The moment has come to enter history, / to suffer the wounds of difference'.

Malroux was born in 1925 in Albi, France, and grew up during the turmoil and aftermaths of two world wars. Of this time, Malroux says, 'I felt I needed to leave a witness, a witness of my youth and my passage in this world. For people to eventually read after me' [This essay was written before Malroux died in February 2025, seven months before her 100th birthday.]. She wrote over a dozen collections of poetry, *La Femme sans paroles* (2006), *Eros* (2006) *Ni si lointain* (2004), *Soleil de jadis* (1998), *Météo Miroir* (2020) and *Reverdir* (2000) among them, and two innovative hybrid texts, *Traces, sillons* (2009) *and Chambre avec vue sur l'éternité* (2005), the latter a faux memoir-correspondence with Emily Dickinson. She also translated Dickinson's poems into French, and writers such as Marilyn Hacker, Henri Cole, Derek Walcott, Saul Bellow, Wallace Stevens, H.D., Anne Carson, Charles Simic, Elizabeth Bishop and Elizabeth Barrett Browning.

As Malroux writes in *Chambre avec vue sur l'éternité*, perhaps in Dickinson's voice, perhaps in her own: 'Remonter le temps, comme on remonte une horloge ou un fleuve', or, 'Going back in time, like turning back a clock or a river'. This is reminiscent of a poem-note by Dickinson that can be found in the archives (along with her botanical specimens, a recipe for cake, a tiny gold ring set with a claret stone) at Houghton Library, Harvard:

> the things of
> which we want
>   the most are those
> we knew before.

'Turning back' and 'knowing before' echo throughout *Daybreak*. For Malroux, writing was an attempt to 'cross time's rapids: necessary provisions', perhaps even halt it – if briefly – altogether, a way to wrench past 'time's ballast'. The collection begins with the elegiac long poem 'Octet for Winter', followed by selections from *A Long-Gone Sun* (2000), *Birds and Bison* (2005) and new poems from 2008 to 2020. Translated by Hacker, there is an ease to the them, thoughtful language choices that make them gleam equally in English as in French. Take the simplicity in this line: 'Et le temps d'une vie le temps s'annule'. With a slight shift in placement, *temps* being *time*, time echoes even closer now: 'And in a lifetime time annuls itself'.

Malroux and Hacker met at a conference of French and American poets in Grenoble in 1989, when Malroux asked Hacker if she would translate one of her poems for a reading because there weren't any translations of her work. They worked together from then on. 'Claire and I would see each other for tea or for lunch and talk about translations and talk about poetry', Hacker explains, 'and Claire would translate some of my poems as well, and we would talk about those too'.

Hacker approaches Malroux's poems as a like-minded confidante. They share similar poetic insights and aesthetics – that is to say, those that work intuitively, gently, attentively. 'I also think that a natural English word order is to be preserved', Hacker explains, 'if there is nothing intentionally strange about the French syntax'. In this poem, for instance:

> Les fenêtres découpent l'abîme
> Les larmes brouillent deux ellipses
> où tout s'échange pour le meilleur et pour le pire,
> le rouge et le bleu
> le present et le passé
> labyrinthe sans issue

And in Hacker's translation:

> The windows frame an abyss
> My tears blur two ellipses
> where everything shifts between better and worse
> red and blue
> past and present
> labyrinth with no exit

Because *abîme* is an *abyss* and *ellipses ellipses*, a chime is naturally uncovered in English. Hacker is also attentive to the vowel sounds in Malroux's line endings – *abîme* and *pire*, *bleu* and *issue*, replicating this stylistic choice when the poem calls for it. *Abyss*, *ellipses*, *worse*, then later, *present*, *exit* – this is exactly what poetry, and poetry in translation, should do – surprise, enhance, connect, transport, help one see what might not otherwise be seen, what has been put aside, hidden, misplaced, forgotten.

Another poem by Malroux:

> Respirent la brise en parlant des incendies
> que des vents (toujours violents) attisent
> dans le (toujours sec) Midi

becomes, in Hacker's hands:

> Inhale the breeze talking of fires
> which (always violent) winds stir up
> in the (always dry) Midi

Maintaining the word *Midi* creates mystery, without being overly obscure or unfamiliar to English readers. A more direct translation of *midi* – *midday* or *afternoon* – would simply fall flat. *Midi* pings around all of the *i* sounds in the stanza. As Malroux says, '[a]t times, the strategy of correspondence works like a bridge. We let some words blur or lose a little of their significance, in order to ensure an enhanced quality'.

In her poems, Malroux externalizes the internal: what is outside turns itself in, and perhaps what is inside turns itself out, suddenly naked, exposed. Like a glove in this poem:

> ... The rectangle
> Swallows the bedroom, it's a different night where
> Life turns inside out like a glove. A veined hand
> Emerges, leaf of a negative
> Hope on the phantom wall.

Or a clitoris in this poem:

> Another is it the same the broad-buttocked female carrying
> her clitoris in front of her like a Périgourdine's bag
> when she goes to market on the village square
> at the hour when the sun gnaws the last bones of snow

What is usually concealed is suddenly, exaggeratingly, uncovered for all to see, an outward display of sexuality that appears both evocative and humorous. In other places, a tender, mannered sensuality slips through, where a woman's 'gently moistened sex' and 'lips' velvet' is juxtaposed with genitals that are 'humbled, shriveled, turning to dust'.

Even a floral arrangement in 'Ballad for a Queen and a Nun' hints at the lurid: 'The rose, lips withered, flaccid flesh, the lily dropping a rosary of aborted seeds that roll down its petals and soil its whiteness'. Unlike Édouard Manet's perfectly painted *Vase de fleurs, roses et lilas* or Berthe Morisot's peonies in a crystal vase, these flowers are past their prime – dying or already dead. Malroux has an eye for decay, a true *nature morte* or *memento mori*. This is reminiscent of Rilke's 'Blaue Hortensie', or 'Blue Hydrangea':

> Just like the last green in a colour pot
> So are these leaves, withered and wrecked
> Behind the flower umbels, which reflect
> A hue of blue only...

There is a Rilkean sensibility to Malroux's poetics, her way of articulating, in precise detail, what she sees, connecting the subject's inner and outer natures at once, in order to give life its most meaningful expression. With this in mind, Malroux brings to light a father's temper, a grandmother's grief, feelings of hunger, sorrow, regret, desire, sadness, pleasure.

Malroux explains her approach to Ricciardi:

> Disons d'abord, et peut-être est-ce une définition qui n'est pas très originale, que pour moi la poésie est essentiellement une tentative pour capter l'invisible. Je la vois surtout comme une moyen d'exploration du monde et de soi-même. Et dans mon esprit, 'soi-même' n'est pas séparé du monde...

> [Let me first say, and perhaps this is not a very original definition, that for me poetry is essentially an attempt to capture the invisible. I see it above all as a means of exploring the world and oneself. And in my mind, oneself is not separated from the world...]

Whether it is a poem that includes images of medieval-tapestry-like hunts filled with millefleur, stags and winged beasts, or this Caravaggio-esque poem (think the paintings *Boy Bitten by a Lizard*, one at the National Gallery, London, one at the Fondazione Roberto Longhi in Florence), about a lizard:

> The wordless woman disowns the hourglass
> Hands crumbling the lizard snatched
> From the wall of its sleep.

Malroux grasps the intimate as well as the intricate and the invisible – a Francis Bacon-like figure washing at a washbasin, a gas oven turned on too long to warm a room, a photo of the writer's face taken in the dark without her knowing. In Malroux's own words: 'They seem to come closer to me in the evening, when the haloed lamp isolates us, a canvas of La Tour or Caravaggio, setting an ambiguous portrait of intimacy in relief...'. Her poetry holds on to the need to delay time 'with a look, a word', where art leads the way towards timelessness:

> This sculpture is
> The only certainty. Today
> Once again, nothing will be decided.

It is also a way of speaking the unspoken. 'The Fires of Absence' details the fragmentary stages of mourning, where '[t]ime is silent' and 'there is no help'. One moment Malroux writes, 'I wait fervently for you to renew and redouble my sentence'. In another, 'Nothing is alive in the city nor precisely dying. Some shops have their shutters lowered, others pretend to open', where, once again, inside and outside are reflections, mirror images, of one another. In this case, neither here nor there, but somewhere in between, like Giotto's frescoes.

One can see a strong visual connection to place throughout *Daybreak*, whether it is the Albi of Malroux's youth:

> Studded with plane-trees
> my southwestern village
> looks like a tree itself, from roots to crown
> tapping the springs of the stream and the main road
> where the two largest shops face each other:
> the café-tobacconist-post-office and the bakery-grocery

with its 'school-gray and church-blue, village-square green and cemetery-white', or Paris, where she latterly lived. In 'Octet Before Winter', Malroux writes, 'The Gare Montparnasse spreads out its entrails / Crossed by an iron bridge in its green cage', the living city taking on anthropomorphic qualities. In other poems, houses have eyes and mouths, trees have fingers that clench into fists when they need to.

There are also catacombs, sepulchres, statues, gravestones, places both alive and dead – 'No need to wait for an apparition', she announces in 'The Shadow at Cabourg'. While in 'Trees of Flames', she writes: 'Death knocks against the mirror, hurls / Brutal shards at the still-living face'. One moment it feels as though she might be walking through Jardin des Plantes, in another, Cimetière du Père-Lachaise. Reading the poem 'On the Use of the Absent', meanwhile, is like looking towards the ornate gold dome of Les Invalides, or the vaulted ceiling at Musée d'Orsay, with its golden rosettes and gilded clock keeping track of time:

> This snow ruffled by the departed
> Beneath the dome of memory
> At hours they choose, but which we also choose
> When our own lives absent themselves

Here, memory is under a cloche, crystalline, celestial, contained, a space where one can look up and see the sun and the sky.

Sunlight, or the impression of sunlight, permeates every surface of *Daybreak*, replenishing the gladiolas and hollyhocks, dahlias and roses that Malroux speaks about, lighting up the darkest corners:

> Still there's a hope:
> Wires might bedeck that jewel box
> With vines and climbing stems to quench
> The eye's thirst, clematis, sweet
> Peas, and why not, morning glories?

And who wouldn't want to walk through this garden:

> the flora has encouraged gold-bellied squash
> elegant artichokes perched on high heels
> blue-green cabbages the colour of eyes and oceans

For Malroux, flowers and plants are significant for their splendour and renewal, her words turning, like tropism, toward warmth and light, no matter the conditions: 'Not with petals but tendrils, fibrils, voluble stems that cling fiercely to life'.

With such vivacity, it is little wonder Malroux's poems resemble paintings. 'We must always revive the imagination', she says. To see an orange-pink sunset the colour of sorbet, or a burst of poppies and lilacs every spring. To see the violet and ochre woods in Paul Sérusier's *Le Talisman, l'Aven au Bois d'Amour* next to the luminous trees in Édouard Vuillard's *Le Jardin des Tuileries* and Maurice Denis's crimson sun in *Tache de soleil sur la terrasse*. In a nearby room, from the late nineteenth century: Marie Bracquemond's ghostly graphite-on-paper *Autoportrait*, Lady Clementina Hawarden's photographic series *Étude d'après nature*, and generations of women in Jenny Girard de Vasson's aristotype *Femmes dans un intérieur, Issoudun*. We read in Malroux:

> Joy: to run barefoot to the window
> and discover daylight there to meet us
> as sure and vibrant as it was yesterday
> to know that nothing has changed or will change
> as long as that light watches over us

and realize that, 'In the furious silence / Lying in ambush in the heart of colour', there is still another day to step into and remember.

Two Poems

NINA BOGIN

Three

The first came in winter
at the year's beginning.
A boy. Stillborn.

Not shown, not touched –
the mother must not attach
herself to the lifeless child.

The father was allowed.
A perfect baby, he said.
Sorrow never mended.

They returned to the house.
Patches of snow,
an empty room.

Then it was spring.
She picked wildflowers
from March until

October, folded
leaves and petals into
notebooks, wrote down

the common names
and Latin names,
the habitats –

meadows, woods,
sunlit or in shade,
torrents' mossy banks.

Month after month
she inscribed herself
into the landscape.

The second came in midsummer,
plucked round
and flushed as a peach,

cloud-soft at her mother's breast.
Slate-blue eyes alert
to the slightest change,

looking at the world, putting
its pieces and people like
a jigsaw together.

Later came an autumn baby.
She pushed herself out, dark hair
sprouting from her head.

Nut-brown eyes, river-deep.
Feisty, apple-hard.
Asleep, sleek as a flower-pod.

She slipped, second
daughter, into the place
made warm by the first.

A family of four. Mother. Father.
Older and younger daughters.
Almost a symmetry.

Two daughters, now grown
with children of their own.
One son, undone.

A shift in the order,
a step aside,
a hare's leap over

the waylaid gift,
still amiss.

The Visitors

You glimpsed them in the white corridors
as I pushed you in the wheelchair.

Over there, your uncles Bruno, Nino.
Then you shook your head, no,

it can't be them, they're dead.
Your grandmother Giulia, you murmured,

touched your arm, spoke your name.
Jean-Pierre, you said. Your closest friend.

How many years had he been gone?
Such a friend you never had again.

And the smallest of them all,
Lorin, our stillborn son.

Perhaps in the quiet of those August days,
he too passed your way.

Reviews

The Return of Close Reading

John Guillory, *On Close Reading*, with an annotated bibliography by Scott Newstok
(University of Chicago Press) £16

Reviewed by Nicolas Tredell

'All respectable poetry invites close reading.' Thus I.A. Richards in a text often seen as a seminal document of twentieth-century Anglophone literary studies, *Practical Criticism* (1929). But what is close reading? John Guillory's 'small book', as his preface calls it – it is really more of an essay padded out by often extensive footnotes and Scott Newstok's useful bibliography – argues that close reading tended to be taken for granted as a core practice of literary study that was little studied in itself, a mode of analysis that went largely unanalysed during the mid-twentieth-century reign of Leavisian criticism in England and New Criticism in the USA. Guillory points out that *Practical Criticism*, despite its use of the term on this one occasion, offers no clear definition nor sustained demonstration of close reading or of the procedures it might entail; his book might more justly be called *Misreading and How To Avoid It*.

In the twenty years that followed the publication of *Practical Criticism*, Guillory observes, the 'term "close reading"' was 'relatively uncommon in the writing of literary critics', conspicuous by its absence 'from the work of William Empson, F.R. Leavis, Cleanth Brooks, W.K. Wimsatt' and others. Some passing references can be traced – Guillory gives examples from Stanley Edgar Hyman, René Wellek and Austin Warren, and John Holloway; but none of these were New or Leavisian critics.

Partly perhaps because of this lack of engagement with close reading as an explicit concept and procedure, there was also a rarely articulated problem with the wider application of a practice that had first emerged as a means of focusing on the short poem, like those Richards used in *Practical Criticism*. How could such a practice cope with longer work – an extended narrative poem, a novel, a play? The practical answer was to treat short sections from longer works as metonymies for the totality of those works, small parts that could supposedly stand for large wholes. As if to try to demonstrate the efficacy of this approach, Cleanth Brooks and Robert Penn Warren's *Understanding Poetry* (1938), which 'came to be regarded as the bible of close reading', was followed by their *Understanding Fiction* (1943), which ducked the difficulty by focusing on short stories rather than novels, and then, with Robert B. Heilman replacing Warren as Brooks's co-author, *Understanding Drama* (1945). But these two later books never attained the authority of the first; they remained in the apocrypha rather than achieving biblical status.

Guillory observes that, ironically, the term 'close reading' began to be more widely used in print as New Criticism and Leavisism started to lose traction. Indeed, its increasing prominence at this time was in inverse proportion to its diminishing influence. Close reading came to be characterized as an enemy to be routed, or an outmoded fashion to be discarded, challenged by rising critical approaches that claimed to be more philosophical (deconstruction), more political (cultural materialism), or more contextual (new historicism). Guillory quotes from 'Against Close Reading', Peter Rabinowitz's 1992 essay: 'close reading is neither the natural, nor necessarily the best way, to approach a text'. Later alternatives include 'hyper' reading, on the model of hyperlinked digital text, 'immersive reading', 'in which the reader is driven constantly forward, without pausing for closer inspection of the text', and 'distant reading', as influentially advocated by Franco Moretti in his 'Conjectures on World Literature' (2000). This last approach was primarily associated with the application of computer analysis to large bodies of texts (the whole corpus of Elizabethan and Jacobean plays and pamphlets, say, or twentieth- and twenty-first-century genre fiction). But this is, as Guillory paraphrases Moretti, the 'dialectical complement of close reading' rather than a replacement for it. Guillory contends that 'our renewed interest in close reading today dates from this moment of distant reading's introduction'.

Close reading 'was propagated by mutual imitation' rather than 'prescription or recipe', and Guillory sees no reason to adopt a different approach. 'It is not necessary for those performing close reading to be able to give a precise verbal account of what they are doing, any more than it is necessary or even possible for musicians or athletes to give a precise verbal account of their performances.' He concludes that 'the disciplinary technique of close reading has an important role to play in response to a media situation revolutionized once again by new technology' – and this role, particularly from a British perspective, recalls the founding moment of Leavisian literary studies, with 'close reading', in league with evaluation, seen as an essential element of a 'minority culture' fighting against 'mass civilization' with its perceived slackening of standards. There can be no return to that moment: but its example retains some pertinence in an era in which social media provide a cushy couch for criticasters and a profitable podium for poetasters.

Adversarial Minds

Ronnie A. Grinberg, *Write like a Man: Jewish Masculinity and the New York Intellectuals*
(Princeton University Press) £30

Reviewed by Tony Roberts

In the October 1968 issue of *Commentary*, Irving Howe published a piece entitled 'The New York Intellectuals: A Chronicle and a Critique', which stamped a name on a loosely affiliated group. Most were Jewish sons of immigrants, anti-Stalinist polemicists who generated as much heat as light. Two years earlier, in *Steady Work*, he had captured their style: 'You argue, you let some heat come through, and you don't pretend that gentility is the ultimate virtue'. Their names are synonymous now with the little literary and cultural journal that gave them a radical platform: *Partisan Review*.

They retain their fascination today as much by the legendary in-fighting as by their combative vigilance through the Depression, the Moscow Trials, the Second World War, the Cold War, Vietnam and, finally, the emergence of a counter-culture that effectively sidelined them. By then they had become insiders, institutional figures, editors and professors. Their ardent left-wing views had either tempered to democratic socialism or migrated right. Republicans listened to the pioneering neoconservatism of some, while a New Left preferred street fighting to the armchair aggression of those who remained liberals.

The first 'generation' of the New York intellectuals was born in the early years of the twentieth century, in tough times. Sidney Hook remembered, 'When I was young, there were three words we dreaded, "diphtheria," because that meant a child would die; "pneumonia," because that meant an adult would die; and "slack," because that meant six months without work.' Alfred Kazin wrote of his boyhood in Brooklyn in *A Walker in the City* (1951), 'I read as if it would fill my every gap, remedy every flaw, let me at last into the great world that was anything out of Brownsville.' In *Making It* (1967), Norman Podhoretz noted the sacrifice required for acceptance beyond the ghetto. A Brooklyn school teacher mentored him, but: 'She was saying that because I was a talented boy, a better class of people stood ready to admit me into their ranks. But only on one condition: I had to signify by my general deportment that I acknowledged them as *superior* to the class of people among whom I happened to have been born.'

A number of the men studied at New York's City College, where tuition was free. They responded to the economic defeat of their parents by becoming intellectual outsiders, finding their voices in *Partisan Review* under editors Philip Rahv and William Phillips. In the late 1930s it developed a hard-nosed style ('raucous, impious, and intransigent' according to Phillips) – a product of their street life and early Marxist training. Or, as Howe once noted, they 'write literary criticism with a strong social emphasis; they revel in polemic; they strive self-consciously to be "brilliant"; and by birth or osmosis, they are Jews'. To Kazin they 'were extremists with a certain Bolshevik habit of mind'. They were literary Modernists also, as Elizabeth Hardwick explained: 'In that circle, the Soviet Union, the Civil War in Spain, Hitler and Mussolini, were what you might call real life but not in the magazine's pages more real, more apposite, than T.S. Eliot, Henry James, Kafka, and Dostoyevski.'

Ronnie A. Grinberg, in her comprehensive and enjoyable *Write like a Man*, tells the story of the New York intellectuals vividly and with an eye to redressing the marginalisation of women involved in the magazines. She sees in masculinity the 'lens' through which to study both male *and* female members (like 'Bloody Mary' McCarthy, Hardwick and Hannah Arendt). For the women writers who made it into *Partisan Review*, the acerbic style they learned led to accusations of coldness that the men never faced.

Grinberg's title comes from Jason Epstein's comment about the sexual appraisal of women contributors. It ends, 'But if a woman could write like a man, that was enough'. To Grinberg, despite the wealth of attention paid to the New York intellectuals, 'few scholars have focused on either gender or Jewishness and the ways in which they intersected in the lives and careers of these figures'. Her contention is that all its members came – 'sometimes consciously' – to 'espouse a secular Jewish masculinity' in their work. (My only reservations about the book are that it wears out the weaponized word 'masculine' and slightly misrepresents itself by the beating it gives its voguish title.)

Write like a Man explores the intellectuals' 'secular ideology' – informed by Freud as well as Marx – with case studies of Diana Trilling, Howe, Midge Decter and Podhoretz. Trilling, middle-class and Radcliffe educated, was recognised as a member of the *Partisan Review* crowd only with her aggressive anti-communism in the 1950s, though she predated other women contributors. They perhaps minded that she also wrote for women's magazines *and* under her husband's name. Lionel Trilling was feted for having caught the *zeitgeist* with *The Liberal Imagination* at a time when, as Louis Menand has commented, the critic's job was to examine literary works for their moral compatibility to the 'correct' political line.

During the war years radicalism gave way to an acceptance of the fact that the *Partisan Review*'s interests and America's were one – except for those committed, like Rahv, to their critical, outsider status. In 1945 the American Jewish Committee founded *Commentary*, edited initially by Elliot E. Cohen, who had helped form the New York intellectuals' ideology as editor of the *Menorah Journal* twenty years earlier. Despite their Cold War anti-communism, the intellectuals found the years of the HUAC dominance difficult to navigate, since they were still viewed with suspicion, whereas ironically they were unwilling bedfellows of McCarthyism and recipients of undisclosed CIA funding.

In-fighting continued. Howe founded *Dissent* in 1954 'to counter what he saw as the excessive conformity of the group and its abdication of the intellectual vocation by celebrating rather than criticizing society'. Although a shoestring enterprise, *Dissent* allowed him to maintain his anti-institutional credentials, while reviewing for *Time* and teaching at Brandeis University.

As with *Partisan Review*, *Dissent* did little to acknowledge the contribution of the women involved. Grinberg makes the point that they 'viewed male-female distinctions as fundamentally and inescapably biological, not social constructions as feminists argued'. This was a position McCarthy, Hardwick and Arendt – born between the 'waves' of feminism – also accepted. Only Trilling eventually modified her position, anticipating in her articles some of the issues in Betty Friedan's *The Feminine Mystique* (1963).

The last two chapters of *Write like a Man* follow the reactionary arc of the careers of Decter, the 'first lady of neoconservatism', and her husband and later Trump apologist, Podhoretz. Decter, a veteran editor (at *Harper's*), became a leading anti-feminist, a critic of women's liberation and the counter-culture, a supporter of 'traditional family values'. She and Podhoretz influenced the conservative establishment's reaction against the militancy of the 1960s and later its hard-line foreign policy. He had studied at Columbia under Trilling and at Cambridge University under F.R. Leavis and would go on to publish *Ex-Friends* (1999), as well as other controversial memoirs.

However divided, the New York intellectuals helped shape the 'broader political, intellectual, and cultural debates in American life up to today'. Grinberg's evidence is in the industriousness of her writers: Howe at *Dissent*; Podhoretz editing *Commentary*; Dwight Macdonald *Politics*; Irving Kristol *Encounter*; Kristol and Daniel Bell *The Public Interest*; the Epsteins starting *The New York Review of Books*.

Flamboyant Coincidence

Ange Mlinko, *Foxglovewise* (Faber) £10.99

Reviewed by Rowland Bagnall

As an asthmatic, I'm sensitive to changes in the air. Though never severely or dangerously difficult, my breathing is affected by humidity and sudden cold, pollen and wood smoke, perfume and cats, cigarettes, aerosol, dust and exhaust fumes. This may explain why my experience of reading *Foxglovewise* was one of noticing its atmospheres, 'thick / and perfumed as an unguent', 'clammy with muscat fug' – where even 'The great refinery of sunset / leaves smoke and bilge in the sky'.

From 'thermal curl[s]' to 'smudgy cigars', Mlinko's poems swirl with thickening agents, the air abuzz, 'electric with bees', flitting with 'Hummingbirds *and* butterflies', the sky, from time to time, amassing monstrous Texan thunderclouds, 'spurting electricity', whipping 'sulfurous wind'. Meanwhile, constant sound and music: whether 'the selfsame / chime' of 'owls and church bells' or the poems' tide of different languages – Greek and Spanish, snatches of Latin, a flurry of 'old Scottish names' – or simply 'the crowd-roar' and 'announcer's commentary' blaring from an airport bar, Mlinko's poetry is a cacophonous environment, where palm trees 'start up like a band in a sudden breeze', flooding 'the gutters of the ears'.

The fullness of the air in *Foxglovewise* brings Bishop's 'Florida' to mind, especially her 'Thirty or more buzzards […] drifting down, down, down', 'like stirred-up flakes of sediment / sinking through water', a viscous, liquid atmosphere, slow and subtropical. A current resident of Florida – 'the state with the prettiest name', according to Bishop – Mlinko appears drawn to the indeterminate nature of the landscape. Indeed, her latest poems (Mlinko's seventh collection, though her first in the UK) are published in the same breath as a new critical monograph, *Difficult Ornaments: Florida and the Poets* (2024), an exploration of the impact of the Sunshine State on a succession of writers for whom 'Florida was an exotic detour', 'sensually intriguing, but also an abstraction that could be worked out in verse'. 'The terrain is always shifting', notes Mlinko in her introduction: 'Poised between drought and flood, gardeners actually water their lawns in the rainy season.'

As with her previous collections, *Foxglovewise* reveals Mlinko to be a restless traveller, roaming from place to place, resistant to permanence. ('[A]re you like the hawthorn tree, / always the same thing in the same place', read lines from Louise Glück's 'Matins', deployed as an epigraph, 'or are you more the foxglove, inconsistent, first springing up / a pink spike on the slope behind the daisies, / and the next year, purple in the rose garden?') Grouped into sections, the poems in this collection are divided by a symbol resembling the prow of an ocean liner, the kind familiar to travel posters from the 1930s. Several of the best poems here take place in Scotland; listening to the *Iliad* on headphones in a rural cemetery, the poet feels as though she stands 'in two foreign countries at once'. Elsewhere, the poems are full of expats and migration routes, charting complex family histories, American myths, alive to the fact that even 'To remember is to cross / Through no-man's-land / Into an imaginary country', to borrow lines from A.E. Stallings, Mlinko's friend and correspondent. In *Foxglovewise*, Mlinko is especially attuned to the relationship between a place and its accruing past, where 'Memories […] surface as a kind of automatism'. As she asks on this collection's final page, 'Are we bound / to the soil we're *born* or *consigned* to?', a relative, perhaps, of Bishop's own question of travel: 'Should we have stayed at home and thought of here?'

For all Mlinko's voyaging, it is the thick, swampy abundance of Florida – its 'disquieting kaleidoscope' of exotic plants and creatures – that takes centre stage. There is a sense of paradox about the place, at once beautiful and slightly gruesome, home to 'voluptuary' hummingbirds and 'emerald frog[s]', shrouded 'in an ecstasy of coastal mist' but also under threat from hurricanes and muddy flooding, trees affected by 'huanglongbing' (a disease producing 'Grotesque oranges'), the fort at Dry Tortugas slowly 'sinking peu à peu'. Bishop's own poem of Florida is tugged between the same extremes, a 'state that floats in brackish water, / held together by mangrove roots / that bear while living oysters in clusters, / and when dead strew white swamps with skeletons', later picturing 'the monstrous, endless, sagging coast-line', 'delicately ornamented'.

And yet, this swampiness creates a pleasing tension in Mlinko's poems, present in her (delicately ornamental?) use of form, her beautifully constructed stanzas, the fluidity of her controlled experiments, her Paul Muldoonesque rhymes and half-rhymes that 'slow the language roaring down the page' (confessor/hairdresser; Miami Zoo/peekaboo). Present, also, are Mlinko's trademark flourishes of unpredictable, flamboyant (i.e. *flamingo-like*) vocabulary, sudden polysyllabic mouthfuls that catch us off-guard; 'amphibrachic', 'melismatic' and 'sacerdotal' surface in the opening poem alone. While these sophisticated structures and (*Write* it!) sesquipedalian encounters can be flummoxing, they are equally delightful and often impressive, like watching the performance of a sculptor or an acrobat. More than this, they seem deliberately to slow the pace of Mlinko's writing – and our reading – to that of the Florida swamp, 'semiotically rich', a reminder that the language of poetry is a thicker substance than the stuff of prose, generating meaning at a different speed.

What the enforced slowness of Mlinko's poetry reveals, to me, is something of the nature of coincidence, the powerful unlikeliness of almost everything that happens, 'Factored into sight by a hair's breadth, / or the turn of the tide': the echoes of history, accidents of evolution, the sheer, surreal coincidence of one word, thought or incident now rhyming with another 'out of magical thin air', a form of enchantment, 'As if / a production of Ariel and Prospero / were pending'. These are difficult and ornate poems, though ones which help us, in the words of Seamus Heaney, to hear 'a music that you would never have known / To listen to', so 'Listen now again'.

Chair and Table

Maurice Riordan, *Selected Poems*, chosen by Jack Underwood (Faber) £14.99

Reviewed by Declan Ryan

This Selected Poems operates on a different basis to that expected – it eschews the usual chronological (or sometimes reverse-order, starting confidently on the newest work) method in favour of an arrangement based on thematic echo, and tone. The editor, Jack Underwood, explains that for him 'a poem takes place outside of time altogether... is durational and always newly becoming'. It is an interesting method, which allows poems to talk to one another in new ways, across decades, and shows Riordan's obsessions and habits to be enduring ones, such as the well-judged list, the turn towards the folkish, the morbid but winking poem of the organism, the tall tale. What is lost by this approach is a sense of the poet's development, the human stuff – to an extent – with poems here about 'Pushing sixty' preceding more puckish, youthful ones. Perhaps one isn't supposed to read a Selected all the way through, anyway, but pick and mix – duck and dive – sampling poems as one-offs, rather than progressions.

Either way, the poems are the thing, and the heart of Riordan's art seems – still – 'The Idylls' from *The Holy Land* (2007), presented here in full. These poems teeter on the verge of prose poetry but are based, on the whole, on a Frostian reported speech, a relaxed tone and phrasing, and present stories of the work in the fields of Riordan's father and other recognisable characters from his personal mythology – Dan-Jo, Moss, The Bo'son – their wit and observations, a matter-of-factness which tightens, at times, into gentle comedy: '"What was a lake for?"/ "God only knows," Moss said. "The Warrens were English"./ "Pleasure, I suppose".' As so often, these are poems which talk quietly of grand ideas, using the local and close-to-hand in order to illustrate the metaphysical, with one memorable poem about the biggest changes seen in the characters' lifetimes ending on a poignant vision which is echoed elsewhere in Riordan's work: '"That", he said, "is my mother on her honeymoon".' The poem immediately before this sequence, here, 'Anniversary', is a movingly terse vision of Riordan's father, 'ripened in death', 'Tonight he will come to me as the young bride / who shyly lifts the counterpane from the dream, / lifts the light cloth and fits himself to my side'.

The twinning, or at least correlation, between desire and death is another of Riordan's preoccupations, whether hearing his mother's voice during an al fresco encounter or an urging to upend, or at least disrupt, domestic comforts in 'During the Recent Thunder & Lightning': 'The incipient desire, then, for catastrophes on a truly grand scale'. This hints at something which becomes clear from experiencing Riordan's work on this larger canvas, and in a new orientation, the sense in which his is a disruptive, genially mischievous voice, one which rightly identifies the Faun as a potential mythic stand-in. Behind these often quiet, or at least down-tuned, poems there is an urge towards non-conformism, devilment and away from cant, or best behaviour – 'Curst be the righteous. Cursed be the whited sepulchres. / Curst be the Just' as 'The Seven Songs of Myself' has it. Notably, one of the angriest – or at least most bracingly polemic – poems here is the only new, uncollected one, 'The Feast of the Holy Innocents'. Riordan isn't one for the head-on collision with the 'political' poem, but his harrowing vision of erasure in the Holy Land brings a certain degree of visceral shock – in or out of context – and adds a new layer to his body of work as a whole – 'the boy half-ripped from his mother painted over as a grain bag; / the boy still gripped by his mother painted over as a wine jug'.

More often, his is a voice which inclines to the gentle ribbing, the 'shoulder tap' school of practical jokes, 'something of a small boy's ingenuity and charm', to take a line from 'The Real Thing'. These are poems which veer between the household ceremony and the urge towards time travel, whether talking of the 'mercy of forgetting' or in conjuring up – invoking, almost – the beloved dead, whether that be family or the way of life of his childhood in rural Cork, its by-ways, landscapes and rhythms, all brought back to life here with an irreverent diligence. In his poem 'Chair' (which here is in between one about a table and one about beds) Riordan writes 'he must learn the virtue / of minimal fuss, to restrain impulse, / to cut irrelevance from the process', and these are words which come to serve, at least in some senses, as his own poetic check-list. Usefully, and cheeringly, he doesn't always follow his own advice – allowing room to break all and any rules, and showing himself across these poems drawn now from five collections, to be adept at surprising the reader, just as he is usually keen to prioritise pleasure, and the 'neglected virtues'.

The Speaking Silences

Philip Gross, *The Shores of Vaikus* (Bloodaxe) £12.00

Reviewed by Hilary Davies

Pine forests. Reed beds. A sea that is not quite a sea. A land that is not quite land. A people who come from many places and from nowhere. Habitations that rise up and sink back into the bog. In Philip Gross's new volume, *The Shores of Vaikus*, all things exist in multiple dimensions. Not least the title. For Vaikus is not a place (or is it?): it is the Estonian word for 'silence'. Also: tranquillity, hush, quietude, stillness, lull, peace, calm, quiet. This is language, and poetry, as shape-shifter.

The roots of this uncertainty lie in Gross's background: his father was a Second World War refugee to Britain, and the post-1945 redrawing of Europe meant that Gross himself did not visit Estonia until well into adulthood. Like so many children of refugees, it was years before he learnt anything but whispers about the traumatic experiences of his father and family. He still speaks the language imperfectly (and it is a daunting language for European non-native speakers to learn, being Uralic, not Indo-European). All of this meant that the country has filled a potent, magical space in his imagination, though when he was finally able to visit after independence he found 'a real, little, ordinary country'. It was almost a relief, 'an entirely positive form of disappointment'.

Nevertheless, that is not the Estonia we encounter in this volume. It is divided into three sections, the central one of which, and much the longest, 'Evi and the Devil', consists of short, evocatory prose paragraphs, which disorientate even as they reveal a winding way through the forest of Estonia's history and geography. Evi is a knowing, elfin, changeling, grown-up child, who not only has an ongoing conversation with the Devil but at times seems both his victim and helpmate. Nasty things happen in the forest, the mushrooms of prehistory are pushed aside by generation upon generation of new, sinister ones, 'coming through the subsoil, ready... to talcum-puff their malevolent spores to the wind'. Gross dabs like a pointilliste, using tricks of light, vegetation and water, gradually building up our realisation of how troubled and troubling this magnificent landscape really is. Vikings, Soviets, Lutherans, Nato fighter jets criss-cross the marshes, airways and seas, none of them Estonian and yet all of them leaving their mark, 'the towers of the Kremlin that way, and New York the other'. No wonder 'we're a shipwreck-raft of souls'.

The other two sections 'sandwich' this unsettling place. The first introduces us to the dizzying expanses of geological time that have created such a distinctive, flat, watery, liminal country. The (beautiful) cover photograph shows us the erratic described in the poem of the same name, 'boulders // as unsure as I am of the down or up of things / reflected. Floating on the surface, on the recumbent sky'. These apparently immovable objects have travelled across the Gulf of Finland, a distance of some 100 miles, and yet the force that moved them, the glaciers, has vanished, like so much else, from this land.

The final section reprises these themes, but now, because of the central prose poems, we are more alert to what they mean: 'History: landscape. Landscape: history... Land made for marching over / by whichever empire now may be in ebb or flow.' The silences of the oppressed and of atrocity merge with, even begin to fade into, the silence of the forest beauty: new growth sprouting from fallen tree trunks, light illuminating the shadows with its own forest, 'There is a forest in the forest... see the sheer trunks of sunlight'. The silence of Vaikus speaks through Gross's evocative and lyric language, which opens for us this enigmatic land of borders.

Pretend

Kate Potts, *Pretenders* (Bloodaxe) £12.99

Reviewed by Charlotte Wetton

Kate Potts's *Pretenders* (Bloodaxe) is a systematic exploration of imposter syndrome. Very much a 'project-book', and informed by academic reading, Potts considers imposter syndrome through mainstream culture, personal experience, art and, above all, through interviews; the majority of the book is made up of verbatim interview text, structured into free verse. As well as the interview poems, there are poems that explore deliberate pretence through people such as Anna Delvey and the eighteenth-century cross-dressing sailor Hannah Snell. A more personal piece is the excellent 'A Telephone Conversation with my Sister/Footnotes'. There's an energising shift in pace and voice between these different types of poems. Potts considers imposter syndrome not only in the workplace, but also across parenting and dating. Reading *Pretenders*, I had that sense that one has in a successful project book, of looking at complexity through differing angles, like a crystal refracting light. The book comes with a thoughtful introduction and notes.

The interview poems see inside others' lives and minds, which is a fascinating privilege. They are very personal and honest pieces. Potts asks the questions we want to ask our friends and colleagues but shy away from. In a meta move, Potts then intervenes her own 'Author' voice and 'Publisher' voice in short prose notes, making transparent her reticence about writing on her own imposter syndrome. I enjoyed the twists and turns of these conversations within conversations. And I found this vulnerability quite moving; *Pretenders* is a courageous book.

Poetry, with its shifting perspectives and multiple voices, is an ideal form for examining a slippery, poorly defined and deeply personal experience such as imposter syndrome. You can sense the interviewees putting the effort into articulating what they've never articulated before (an implicit comment on the limitations of language but more interesting to read than most poetry that attempts to do this.) In doing so, Potts has created a book that is likely be genuinely helpful to people (unlike, one must admit, most poetry books).

But *Pretenders* is not without its weaknesses. Potts acknowledges in the introduction that she has tried and largely failed to reach beyond her own circle to find interview participants (it is a difficult thing to do). The eleven interviews are rather narrowly concentrated around the health, artistic and academic professions, and there are more women than men. This has an aesthetic implication because we experience a narrower range of experience and voice, especially as the same interviewees reappear.

The larger aesthetic issue with the interview poems is that Potts just has not done enough with her found text. While I respect her decision to be faithful to the verbatim text, her editorial interventions are sparser than they ought to be. The free verse spacing of the interview poems successfully recreates the hesitations and silences of natural speech – particularly speech on a difficult topic – and the white space makes them easy to read and follow. However, I was unconvinced by Potts's line breaks, and some of the interview poems unsuccessfully attempt stricter forms. At 123 pages, the book struggles to retain our interest *as poetry*. We don't read poetry for information; we read it to be within an experience. 'Poems exist to foreground the event of their language', as James Longenbach has written. My issue with *Pretenders* is that I would revisit it out of an interest in imposter syndrome, but I wouldn't revisit it out of an interest in the language.

Still, Potts's book is a bracing read. Perhaps we are shaking off the Romantic notion of the individual writer blessed with divine inspiration in favour of a more co-produced aesthetic as well as ethic. It might be a way of writing that avoids both the nihilism of 'post-truth' and the elitism of old certainties. Is it not courageous, too, for a writer to admit that they don't have all the answers, that they're seeking, not only other perspectives and insights, but others' language?

Looking backwards to go forwards

Katrina Porteous, *Rhizodont* (Bloodaxe) £12.99; Stephen Sawyer, *Carrying a Tree on the Bus to Low Edges* (Smokestack) £7.99

Reviewed by Sarah-Clare Conlon

At a reading series I frequent, performing poets are advised that preambles should not outrun the pieces themselves. True, but complex constraints and processes require explanation, and extracts of a wider project or residency demand context. Sometimes we need to be shown the bigger picture.

Katrina Porteous gives us an entire gallery tour. With four pages of introduction, a further thirty pages of endnotes and acknowledgements, and reams of footnotes, I feared being overwhelmed. Confident, knowing the existence of collaborations and commissions, audio sequences (Porteous being known for her 'radio-poetry') and responses to scientific research, I ditched flicking back and forth, and dug in.

Straight off, I was grabbed by the glowworms of 'Tiny Lights' – 'Mysterious in the twenty-first century – alien, ancient' – as mesmerised as the observers who 'waited, like brigands, for the dark' but who are dragged back to the present day as 'Not a mile away, a police siren wailed'. We encounter much in the way of nature through *Rhizodont*: dragonflies, hedgehogs, hermit crabs, anemones, orchids, 'gigantic ferns / And spidery horsetails', 'Painted Ladies' butterflies 'Flickering from knapweed to thistle-top, they rise', seasonal 'Sand Martins', 'their little blunt faces / Bursting into the light'.

The pages are teeming with birds, from the domesticated stobbies and skyemmies pigeons (reminiscent of Liz Berry's lilting 'Birmingham Roller') to the wild visitors, often given their Northumbrian names, such as the tern (tirrick, tarree, teerum, pickie) and the eider: 'Cubby, ye're a bonny bord. Mild, an' ower-soft, / Wallerin' doon the ooze wi' yer sea-byet feet' (*'Eider, you're a good-looking bird. Mild, and so soft / Waddling down on the mud with your sea-boot feet'*, my translation). Yet the natural world is not always beautiful and, despite highlighting the plight of certain species, the writing at times errs towards the sentimental and feels as though it is passing judgement.

Dialect plays a central role, particularly in Book I: Carboniferous, a 'journey through the sedimentary landscapes of England's North-East coast', where it contributes to creating an aural experience as well as to expanding (and experimenting with) language. Certain passages conjure vivid images of being recited aloud – 'A Hut A Byens' ('a heap of bones'), especially – others function as songs or even sea shanties – '*A hobble, a wabble, a bit of top rabble*' of 'Arguments', for example, with its 'seven old fishermen in a smoky hut'. Some of the poems offer a call-and-response feel, echoing lines, phrases and words previously encountered; the repetition also adds an ebb and flow reminiscent of the shoreline we're taken to.

People are ever present, too, and I was compelled to return to the long poem 'A Lang Way Hyem', which borrows from real-life interviews conducted with locals and holidaymakers overlooking Beadnell Harbour, and which ends with an interesting contrapuntal and the instruction 'Whisper'. With varying voices, and subtly worked as well as internal rhymes, reminiscent of Dylan Thomas's *Under Milk Wood* or *Dart* by Alice Oswald, I feel I'll be back to this one again.

Carrying a Tree on the Bus to Low Edges is Stephen Sawyer's second collection with Smokestack, and one of the last to roll off Andy Croft's production line (see *PNR* 280 for more on the press, which, incidentally, published Katrina Porteous's Northumberland epic *Dunstanburgh*).

The Low Edges of the title are in Sheffield, where Sawyer lives, and the city's places and people are captured in these pages. Pay attention to the names, as you'll meet some of them more than once, including a horse going by the name of Lottie and a pub (with a chequered history, the CAMRA website tells me) called the Sheaf View.

The long poem of that name paints a colourful, busy scene therein on 'the first cold night / of the winter', intersperses found text with snatches of overheard conversations with snapshots of the punters, from printmakers and pet groomers to 'film students / who film students': 'Rivulets / of condensation, a slow / motion butchery of faces / in the window night'. There's even a ghost dog.

Apparitions are apparent throughout, as death and fate are approached in light of the pandemic. This is largely a lockdown book, reminding us of those symbols and phrases we thought we'd never unsee or unhear, but five years on we've largely forgotten, save for the odd footprint ghost signs forming an orderly queue on the pavement outside a post office.

In '1.5 Metres of Earth', our narrator's sense of reality seems to be spiralling out of control: '"Pandemic" / becomes "panic", your body and words, my body / and words'. This dream sequence feeling is reflected in the typography tail-spinning about the page, as the words zip by questioning, repeating – 'It's hard to know what normal is' – getting dizzy from going round in ever-decreasing, nonsensical circles: 'feel like a masked ball / in a secret room that contains / all masked balls in all secret –'.

Repetition is effective in bringing back the various mantras 2020 taught us – we're up and down staircases, constantly in exile, never not thinking about time, never not thinking about place and space: 'Time dissolving into place'; 'The space around me is next of kin. / I am a sieve of time within time, / previous and subsequent presents, / nameless spaces within places'. Even the spirit of 'Proust's madeleines dunked in tea, his fragile / enduring memory' is invoked for the purpose of exorcism. Perhaps that's one of the book's strengths – it helps us exorcise the lost years, helps us to forget having been the ones 'wearing a hat like a lid / on a scream'.

I Shook My Head

Ella Frears, *Goodlord: An Email* (Rough Trade Books) £14.99

Reviewed by Jazmine Linklater

Renters across the UK will be familiar with Goodlord, the online 'property technology' platform which removes what little human interaction there had been in the administration of tenancy. When Ella Frears's own lettings agent demanded she make a Goodlord account, she was filled by 'a strange, chilled anger'. So she did what any goodly bureaucratic subject must: she wrote an email.

This memoir-novel-poetic sequence's sing-song rhythms carry narrative into all sorts of knotty and depraved scenarios. From its opening 'Dear Ava', *Goodlord: An Email* spools out memories, anecdotes and jokes about the various spaces the speaker has rented over the years, from The Big House of dreams through student halls, a basement flat and various house shares to artist residencies in museums and houses and gardens between periods of sofa surfing. Spaces stack up while the narrative hurtles towards Boatswain's Clench (a comically unappealing name) and the events that unfold there on her first artist's residency. Frears is a master joke teller and *Goodlord* is funny as hell, unceasingly bawdy and oftentimes candid, but also capable of classic romcom, as in her arrival at her Boatswain's Clench residency: fresh from the city with her 'suitcase, miniskirt, / impractical boots with a little heel', scuttling along 'through the forest, along the river, down the road' for miles to her accommodation. Fresh from years of cramped and tormenting living conditions, she predictably has no idea what to do with herself in the idyllic little studio she's been gifted for eight weeks: her focus settles on the modes of spooky surveillance she's plagued by.

There's an actual ghost in her mostly closed-down out-of-season B&B, where she's not only pressured into cooking for the landlady but catering for the two other guests (here especially, as throughout, I'm reminded of Holly Pester's brilliant novel *The Lodgers*, both speakers defaulting pitiably to frying single eggs when freed from the requirement to perform dining for others). She watches the B&B's CCTV footage like the telly, watches the Chairman of the Trust roam around the woods while keeping tabs on her, watches ex-army boat-building student Martin Cooper circling like a vulture. The way Frears layers increasingly sinister events with casually detached humour makes it hit home so much harder when (spoiler alert) she learns that a local woman's murder by a jealous partner took place just outside her bedroom. This in turn becomes just one instance in an unceasing roll call of instances of violence against women – from lads' daily banter ('you've got to laugh, Ava, you know that, we know that'), through attempted sexual assaults that are brushed off ('thank god for the sturdy weave of a good quality gusset!'), to normalising the experiences through humour as the only available path to utterance: 'I guess eventually the words detach – become sayable – / matter of fact', until this system fails. When deeply upsetting experiences of serious sexual assault occur the speaker has no language: '*you're going to tell me you were raped or something?'* // I shook my head. / I didn't say a thing'.

But this book does more than account for the banality of violence against women. It's about how we (women, yes, but also all of us) are inculcated into structures of power, how we're abused by them and complicit in them – gender and sexuality, capital, property, and even Poetry (yes, capital P). The rolling rhythm combined with the repeated use of apostrophe to the lettings agent, Ava, makes a joke of theorised lyric triangulation through the relation at hand: 'It's always been a triangle – us, / and you, the shapeless, shadowy fork that is / our landlord'. The speaker is haunted by snippets of school-enforced Poetry by Eliot and Frost and Hardy ('fuck off Hardy'), so she weaponises them wickedly, glibly, quoting Yeats's 'The Second Coming' in the middle of an interrogation of which sorts of porn people are into. *Goodlord* reaches for methods of debasing gatekeepers, the upholders of power structures, Ava and Eliot alike. She can't quote any women poets here because the emergent sexuality the book recounts is formed in and by heteropatriarchy – as is her relationship to Poetry, and property, and everything else that governs her.

Because what this text is good at is exhibiting, if not elucidating, the messed-up way young women often learn to yearn for their own sexualisation ('I liked how I became the centre of the orbit... all glances led to me / my body. / Hot.') long before they realise the danger they're already courting ('Ava, I know this sounds so stupid, / but I thought I had it covered'). *Goodlord* is raging *and* delusional, and Frears unabashedly treads this line between fantasy and fetish, its bad-faith romanticisation of the sexy waitress who gets constant surface-level gratification but somehow still finds herself superior to it all. And if Frears preaches to the choir, rehashing the things our generation repeatedly says to itself, or lays explanation on a bit thick, we forgive her. Seeing a baby bird in the middle of a footpath she has the overwhelming urge to touch it: 'And I realised, Ava, that the way that I was looking / at this frozen, frightened bird, / was the way that men / in cars and on the street had looked at me when I was in / my uniform walking home from school'. How valuable it is that she *has* laid this all out so plainly and so readably! Sometimes what we really need from a book is a good pal whose frank, funny description of our own lives means we can see clearly our involvement in the structures that govern them.

Concrete Flowers

The Collected Poems of Mary Ellen Solt, edited by Susan Solt (Primary Information) $24

Reviewed by Greg Thomas

Mary Ellen Solt is best remembered as the editor of the 1968 anthology *Concrete Poetry: A Worldview*, the most authoritative of the various compendiums of concrete poetry that appeared during the late 1960s. As her daughter Susan Solt notes in an afterword to the present volume, that anthology, which includes a series of lucid prose statements by its editor, remains Mary Ellen's 'signature work of scholarship'.

The poem adorning the cover of *Concrete Poetry: A Worldview*, Solt's telegraphic acrostic 'Forsythia' (reproduced in the present volume), might seem to signal gentle dissent against the hard-edged linguistic abstraction that held sway across much of the book's contents. Concrete poetry in the classic sense had been coded as minimalist, anti-expressionist, perhaps above all non-pictorial. Yet here was a flowing, floral paean preserving both the rhythm of demotic speech and the figurative possibilities of visual poetics.

The title word 'FORSYTHIA' is spelled out in serifed capitals across the base of the visual frame, with a further word blossoming upwards from each letter: 'Forsythia Out Race Springs's Yellow Telegram Hope Insists Action'. beyond the terminus of each word, the opening letter reaches still further upwards in a wavey petal shape, repeated in between iterations of its morse-code equivalent, a coded reference (literally) to the metaphor of the forsythia as a telegram, breaking the news of the returning sun. This beautiful poem was part of a series, *Flowers in Concrete*, first published as a portfolio of letter-pressed posters in 1966 by the Fine Arts Department at the University of Indiana, where Solt spent most of her life, teaching while raising a family with her husband, the historian Leo Solt.

In 2010, a special issue of *OEI* magazine was dedicated to Solt's critical writing. This made clear that Solt's concrete poetics was rooted in a deep scholarly appreciation of William Carlos Williams's work – latterly a close friend – in particular of his emphasis on word placement as a means of transcribing the North-American demotic. This was quickened by Solt's technical musical training and love of classical performance. As Susan Solt notes in her afterword, 'this gave her unique insight through musical structure into Williams's search for the American idiom... Her musical lexicon and her ear for tempo and rhythm infused both her linear and concrete poems.'

If the 2010 publication revived Solt's status as a critic of concrete and post-objectivist poetics, the present volume does the same for her largely lost poetic oeuvre. And the results are a joy to behold. Solt appears here as a poet of musical dexterity, subtle formal daring, and abiding faith in the cyclical rhythms of nature and redemptive possibilities of human connection. Among other things, it would be possible to focus on the myriad ways in which Solt adapts concrete and post-objectivist idioms to the complexities of female experience.

In the very first poem in the collection, 'With Child', Solt whimsically embraces before violently expelling the woman-as-nature metaphors that came as a burden of pregnancy: 'if I am the sky where a / wing beats / the sea where a // fish swims / in my forever / why is it I / want to vomit / the thing'. Elsewhere, in 'Child with Magazine', which reads, in sum, 'Mommy, / what does / L I F E / spell?', the author is surely nodding to a famous concrete poem by Décio Pignatari in which the four letters L, I, F, and E form the basis of a kinetic permutation poem. That piece is here restaged, as it were, in a domestic sphere where life, through replete with creative possibilities, also comes freighted with invisible labour and the exigencies of child rearing.

In her 1985 prose piece 'Notes on a Letter from William Carlos Williams', Solt records her determination during the early 1960s to 'make poetry of my woman's life'. But to reduce this collection to ballast for revisionist histories of avant-garde poetics would be to do it a disservice. We should also acknowledge, for example, the ways in which Solt's concrete poetry responds to contemporaneous semiotics, as in non-semantic sequences such as 'Marriage: A Code Poem'. Contemporary politics make an appearance in the witty and acerbic placard poems of *People Mover: A Demonstration Poem* (1968), where downward-facing A's and exclamation marks become incendiaries raining down Yankee justice on the citizens of Vietnam. Elsewhere, as in the hand-lettered 'Dogwood' sequence and the late sequence 'Kairos', envisaging Mary's journey to the birthplace of Christ, a mystical and – we sense – deeply humane spirituality makes its mark.

Perhaps above all, these are poems about nature and the elements: rain, snow, waterfalls, stones making ripples in ponds like parentheses (as in 'Untitled [so swift]'). Solt's work is at its most enchanting when a lucid visual pictography evoking scene and atmosphere is combined with a Williams-esque feel for the page as score: where visual form becomes both rhythm and diagram. Then, truly, she flowers in concrete.

Some Contributors

Alberto Manguel is a Argentine-Canadian writer, translator and critic. From 2025 to 2018, he was the director of the Argentine National Library. He is now the director of 'Espaço Atlântida: Centro de Estudos da História da Leitura' in Lisbon.

Csilla Toldy published three poetry pamphlets with Lapwing, Belfast. Her collection *Firebird* is forthcoming with Arlen House in 2025. Recent poetry and translations appeared in Southword, Cyphers, MPT, HLO and Asymptote.

Declan Ryan's debut collection, *Crisis Actor*, was published in 2023.

Dick Davis's publications include volumes of poetry and verse translation chosen as books of the year by *Sunday Times* 1989; *Daily Telegraph* 1989; *Economist* 2002; *The Washington Post*, and *The Times Literary Supplement* 2013 and 2018.

Greg O'Brien is an artist and writer based in Wellington, New Zealand, Gregory O'Brien's most recent collection of poems is *House & Contents* (Auckland University Press 2022). An exhibition of his paintings and poems was exhibited at the Manchester Poetry Library early in 2024.

Greg Thomas is the author of *Border Blurs: Concrete Poetry in England and Scotland* (Liverpool UP, 2019) and co-editor, with Julie Johnstone, of a forthcoming selected edition of Edwin Morgan's concrete poetry (Reaktion, 2026).

Hilary Davies's fifth collection, *Compass Light*, is forthcoming from Renard Press in autumn 2025. She has been an RLF Fellow at King's College, London and the British Library. In 2023 she was shortlisted for the Michael Marks Environmental Poet of the Year award.

Jena Schmitt's poems, short fiction, essays and drawings have appeared in publications in the UK, Canada and the US.

Mary O' Malley was educated in Galway University and has taught English and Writing in Ireland, the US and in mainland Europe. Her most recent collection, *The Shark Nursery*, was published by Carcanet (2024). She has received a number of awards in the US, in Spain and Ireland. She is working on new poems and a collection of prose.

Nell Prince is a poet from Lincolnshire. She is the 2025–26 Harper-Wood studentship recipient.

Nina Bogin lives in eastern France. Her most recent poetry collection is *Thousandfold* (Carcanet). Her translation of Agota Kristof's *The Illiterate* (*L'analphabète*) appeared with CB Editions and New Directions.

Richard Gwyn's most recent books are the memoir *Ambassador of Nowhere: A Latin American Pilgrimage* (Seren) and his translations of Fabio Morábito's poetry, *Invisible Dog* (Carcanet). He is the author of the Substack newsletter *Raids on the Underworld*.

Rowland Bagnall's second collection, *Near-Life Experience* (2024), was an Observer Poetry Book of the Month. A selection of his writing is available online: www.rowlandbagnall.com

Sarah-Clare Conlon's fifth limited-edition pamphlet *Wanderland* (Red Ceilings Press) is a Poetry Book Society Summer 2025 Listing and has been nominated for the Wainwright Prize.

Sasha Dugdale won the 2025 Anglo-Hellenic League Runciman Award for *The Strongbox* (Carcanet, 2024).

Tony Roberts has published five collections of poetry, including *The Noir American* (2018), and three books of essays on poets, critics and biographers. The latest, *A Movement of Mind*, appeared last year. His work is published by Shoestring Press. He also contributed an essay to *Robert Lowell in Context*, edited by Austenfeld and Kość for Cambridge University Press (2024).

Uilleam Blacker is a literary scholar and translator based in University College London. His translations have appeared in, among others, *Guardian*, *White Review*, and *Modern Poetry in Translation*.

Zoe Skoulding's latest collection is *A Marginal Sea* (Carcanet, 2022). She is Professor of Poetry and Creative Writing at Bangor University and lives on Ynys Môn/Anglesey.

Hal Coase is currently the Harper-Wood Student at St John's College, Cambridge. His first collection, *Eccolo*, is published by Carcanet this July. He lives in Rome.

Trinidadian Scottish writer **Anthony V. Capildeo** FRSL is Professor at the University of York. In 2025, their work was recognized with the Windham-Campbell Prize and the Bocas Litfest Prize for Poetry.

Robyn Marsack is writing an account of her grandparents' lives during the First World War. She edited Edmund Blunden's war prose *Fall in, Ghosts* and *Selected Poems* for Carcanet.

WWWW.PNREVIEW.CO.UK

Editors
Michael Schmidt
John McAuliffe

Editorial Manager
Andrew Latimer

Contributing Editors
Anthony Vahni Capildeo
Sasha Dugdale
Will Harris

Copyeditor
Maren Meinhardt

Designed by
Andrew Latimer

Editorial address
The Editors at the address on the right. Manuscripts cannot be returned unless accompanied by a stamped addressed envelope or international reply coupon.

Trade distributors
Combined Book Services Ltd

Represented by
Compass IPS Ltd

Copyright
© 2025 Poetry Nation Review
All rights reserved
ISBN 978-1-80017-474-0
ISBN 0144-7076

Subscriptions—6 issues
INDIVIDUAL–print and digital: £45; abroad £65
INSTITUTIONS–print only: £140; abroad £162
INSTITUTIONS–digital only: from Exact Editions (https://shop.exacteditions.com/gb/pn-review) to: PN Review, Main Library, University of Manchester, Oxford Road, Manchester, M13 9PP, UK

Subscriptions & Enquiries:
support@pnreview.co.uk

Supported by